POLITICAL BEHAVIOR

$$\underline{\Sigma \in \infty\ \mu \leq \exists\ \forall\ \mho}$$

**Abdul Karim Bangura
Dawit Isayas
Gerald Smith
Michael O. Thomas**

University Press of America, Inc.
Lanham • New York • London

NOTABLE

Copyright © 1996 by
The African Institute
University Press of America,® Inc.
4720 Boston Way
Lanham, Maryland 20706

3 Henrietta Street
London, WC2E 8LU England

All rights reserved
Printed in the United States of America
British Cataloging in Publication Information Available

Library of Congress Cataloging-in-Publication Data

Political behavior / Abdul Karim Bangura...(et al.).
p.   cm.
Includes bibliographical references and index.
1. Political culture. 2. Political participation. 3. Political psychology. 4. Political sociology. I. Bangura, Abdul Karim.
JA75.7.P646   1996   306.2--dc20   95-39480 CIP

ISBN 0-7618-0222-3 (cloth: alk. ppr.)
ISBN 0-7618-0223-1 (pbk: alk. ppr.)

JA75.7 .P646 1996

0134107655497

Political behavior /

c1996.

2005 05 09

⊖™The paper used in this publication meets the minimum requirements of American National Standard for information Sciences—Permanence of Paper for Printed Library Materials, ANSI Z39.48—1984

Dedication

To Our Students

Contents

Acknowledgements	vii
Preface	ix
Chapter 1 An Interaction Theorem of Political Context	1
Chapter 2 Exchange Structure	7
Chapter 3 Action Structure	29
Chapter 4 Ideational Structure	51
Chapter 5 Participation Framework	91
Chapter 6 Information State	109
Bibliography	145
Indices	155
About the Authors	164

Acknowledgements

To acknowledge our indebtedness to the many scholars upon whose works we have drawn in writing this book would be impossible, the more so since we would run the risk of unwittingly leaving out some whose contributions to aspects of political behavior have been no less important. The citations in each chapter and the Bibliography at the end of the book will, we trust, give some indication of our debt to past and contemporary scholars on aspects of political behavior.

We would, nevertheless, like to recognize the following colleagues who have been particularly generous in various ways: Professors Nathanael Pollard, Jr., Esther E. Ward, Ralph Parris, Mario Fenyo, Zak Kondo, William Lewis, M. Sammye Miller, Joseph Kum, Lavonne Jackson, Ganamuthu Wilson, Abiy Tsegaye, Francis Simbo, Hannah Dagnachew, John Otto, Winston Murray, and Mekonen Haddis. Their kind assistance has substantially improved many aspects of our treatment. We take this opportunity to thank them for their interest.

We would also like to extend our sincere gratitude to our family members (in the African sense) without whom the completion of this book would have been impossible. They gave encouragement and displayed considerable forbearance during our preoccupation with this work.

Last, but certainly not least, we want to express our indebtedness to our students, both past and present, who have all contributed in one way or another to clarifying our thinking on a number of problems as a result of many interesting and stimulating discussions on matters of political behavior. It is to them we gratefully dedicate this book.

Abdul Karim Bangura
Dawit Isayas
Gerald Smith
Michael O. Thomas

Preface

Although political scientists often stress the concept of *political behavior*, few make explicit the methodology used either for its discovery or for its incorporation into an analysis. This book poses a model of political behavior and suggests that particular expressions provide clues about where citizens locate their behaviors within the contexts defined by this model.

Many branches of political science have stressed the influence of political contexts on citizens' political behaviors. *Political theory* focuses on how ethical, empirical, and prudential issues affect political behavior. *Comparative politics* looks at how different communities--usually nations--affect political behavior. *International politics* examines how relations between nations and of such global organizations as the United Nations influence political behavior. *American politics* studies how the American community conducts its public business at the national, state, and local levels and its effects on political behavior. *Public administration and public policy* focus on the formulation and appraisal of domestic and foreign policy and their effects on political behavior. This proliferation of contexts can certainly place anyone who argues for a decontextualized political science on the defensive. However, there is a problem inherent in the conclusion that so diverse a set of vague and general contexts can influence political behavior. How can one know precisely which contexts have influenced a citizen's political behavior and the political analyst's interpretation of a political behavior? In other words, how can political analysts move from the **POSSIBLE** contextual influences on political behavior to an understanding of the **ACTUAL** contextual influences on political behavior. These questions are important because each branch of political science previously mentioned has incorporated some notion of political context into its theoretical explanations and models of political behavior, without always making explicit either their methodological route toward its discovery, or what is to be included within a context once it enters into an analysis.

In this book, the focus is on **THE POLITICAL BEHAVIORS OF VOTERS AND REPRESENTATIVES WHICH INFLUENCE THE PRODUCTION AND INTERPRETATION OF A POLITICAL CONTEXT WITHIN A POLITY**. By using the term *political context*, we intend to place greater emphasis on how surrounding behaviors contribute to context than on the contribution of voter/representative identities, economic situations, social situations, or cultural constructs. By using the voter and the representative as major units of analysis, it is presupposed in this book that the ideal political system is a *representative democracy*. This concept is most concisely stated by Joseph Schumpeter (1950:269): "The democratic method is that institutional arrangement for arriving at political decisions in which individuals [i.e. leaders] acquire the power to decide by means of a competitive struggle for the people's vote." Whenever the word "democracy" is employed in this book, it will have the meaning assigned to it by Schumpeter.

This book is divided into six chapters. In chapter one, an interaction theorem of political context that shapes political behavior is introduced. The subsequent chapters (two through six) elaborate the various levels of structure of political context: exchange structure, action structure, ideational structure, participation framework, and information state.

The individuals who will read this book will be engaged in the politics of the twenty-first century. They will have to be prepared to step forward and respond effectively, intelligently, and humanely to the political issues of that time. This book, which seeks to introduce readers to political behavior from a voter-representative perspective, is an attempt to help them respond to those future problems with wisdom and comprehension.

Chapter 1

An Interaction Theorem of Political Context

The Context of Politics

Because the significance of voters' and representatives' political action is doubly contextual in being both **context-shaped** (its contribution to on-going sequence of political actions cannot adequately be understood except by reference to the context in which it is undertaken) and **context-renewing** (the character of political actions is directly related to the fact that they are context-shaped--the context of a next political activity is repeatedly renewed with every current action), **context** then helps an analyst to rule out unintended activities and suppress misunderstandings of certain activities that take place in a political arena. In essence, those factors identified as contextual must be those that determine the voters' and representatives' actions and interpretation of those actions in actual political activities. In order to explain the context of politics, the following theoretical framework outlines a model with five different levels of structure. The subsequent discussion explicates these structures.

Political Context: A Theoretical Framework

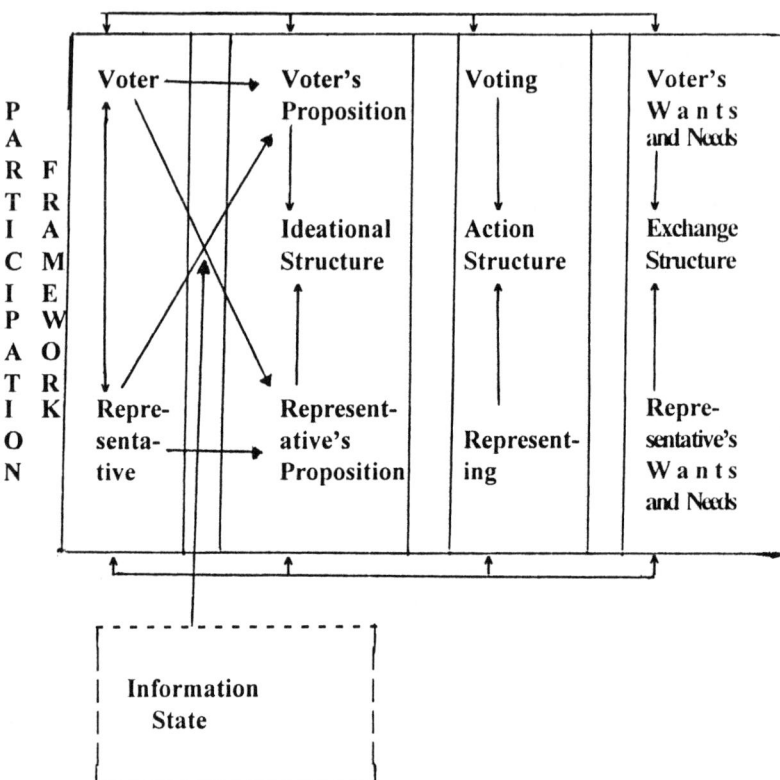

Propositions

P_1: Political domains involve conceptually distinct local contexts for each political transaction. It is these contexts to which politics provides a pathway--and thus, these contexts are the ones a political analyst can discover through analyzing voters' and representatives' use of politics.

P₂: Although many analysts often stress the concept of **POLITICAL CONTEXT**, none has made explicit the methodology used either for its discovery or for its incorporation into analysis.

1. **Exchange Structure**: This is the result of the decision procedures by which a voter and a representative alternate their sequential needs (necessities) and wants (desires) and define those alternations in relation to each other. The structure is critical in fulfilling the system constraints of politics.

2. **Action Structure**: This is the outcome of directing attention to orders or occurrences and to the decision procedures through which such orders come to be. Thus, the function of voting (looking for and evaluating candidates) and representing (promoting the interests of constituents) occur in constrained linear sequences: they are not randomly ordered; there is a pattern and a predictability to their occurrences. Voting and representing are therefore situated in a political arena, such that what counts as a particular action is strongly constrained by what action structure is important for fulfilling ritual constraints; that is, the interpersonal requirements of voting and representing.

3. **Ideational Structure**: This can be seen as the result of the voters' and representatives' roles in negotiating their propositions for ideas, services, and goods. Three different relations between ideas contribute to the overall configuration of the ideational structure: (a) **Cohesive Relations** are established when a voter and a representative interpret an element in one proposition from a prior proposition because of the political relationship underlying them. (b) **Topic Relations** concern what a voter and a representative actually talk about on a given political transaction. (c) **Functional Relations** concern the roles ideas play in relation to one another and within the overall political context. For example, in a political district, some ideas for the quality of a particular representative or voter may serve as a descriptive background for the quality of other representatives and voters.

4. **Participation Framework**: This refers to the fact that when a political transaction is taking place, a voter and a representative who happen to be in a perceptual range of the event will have some sort of participation status relevant to it. The codification of these various positions and the normative specification of appropriate conduct within each provide an essential background for political interaction. The combination of voter and representative participation statuses, and the norms specifying appropriate conduct within these statuses, make up the participation framework. Thus, participation frameworks can be altered by changes in political transactions--individuals' alignment to self and other as expressed in the way they handle such transactions.

5. **Information State**: Although voters and representatives again play a central part, they do so not in their social interactional capacities, but in their cognitive capacities. This cognitive focus hinges on the fact that an information state involves the organization and management of **knowledge** (what a voter knows and what a representative knows about ideas, services, and goods) and **metaknowledge** (what a representative and a voter know about their respective knowledge of the ideas, services, and goods in question). One should also note that there is an interactional relevance to knowledge and metaknowledge: the transaction of voting and representing signifies the exchange of information, knowledge and metaknowledge are constantly in flux, and information states are constantly evolving over a course of a transaction. And since information states are interactively emergent, they can become pragmatically relevant so long as representatives and voters display their knowledge and metaknowledge about ideas, services, and goods to one another.

Conclusion

It is evident from the preceding discussion that voters and representatives are interactionally related in a participation framework, and their knowledge and metaknowledge about ideas, services, and goods are organized and managed in an information state. All of these structures provide a framework within which any single political transaction is produced. Although integrated in a political arena, these structures are conceptually distinct local contexts for each political transaction; that is, local political domains in which a transaction is situated. It is these contexts to which politics provides a pathway--and thus, these contexts are the ones which an analyst can discover through analyzing voters' and representatives' use of politics.

Chapter 2

Exchange Structure

Introduction

In the preceding chapter, we defined *Exchange Structure* as the result of the decision procedures by which voters and representatives alternate their sequential needs (necessities) and wants (desires) and define these alternations in relation to each other. We also mentioned that this structure is critical in fulfilling the system constraints on politics. As such, the rest of the discussion in this introductory section deals with the conceptualization and underlying principle of exchange. After that, the remainder of the chapter looks at the myth about political exchange; a definitive and descriptive approach to understanding what is meant by exchange structure; the state as an instrument, agent, and suitor of exchange and as policy-maker responsible for the allocation and distribution of resources. Finally, concerns are raised to discuss various problems with global political accountability in terms of global expectations of exchange.

Political Exchange can be defined as an act of reciprocal giving and receiving between voters and representatives. Given this definition, we advance the following proposition:

P_3: If voters and representatives have differing marginal rates of substitution[1], all can be made better off in the sense of attaining a more preferred level of benefit by exchange.

Put more realistically in terms of politics, Senator Z is willing to exchange his/her vote on Senator Y's legislation for a government-financed project that will satisfy Senator Z and his/her constituents. If s/he is willing to trade more than one vote on a number of legislation that will make him/her and a great majority of his/her constituents happier, all will be made better off by the exchange. The same analysis can be applied to any other type of exchange in the political arena. Thus, exchanges occur in the political arena when voters' and representatives' rates of substitution are not equal.

The Myth about Political Exchange

Political exchange, as mentioned earlier, involves giving up one thing for another. Thus, a popular myth is that the exchange of a vote or a policy for another is a zero-sum game in which one group of voters' and/or representatives' gain is necessarily a loss to another.

However, voluntary political exchange is productive for at least three reasons. First, it channels resources to those who need them most. A legislation that helps tobacco growers in North Carolina will be of no use to non-smokers in Alaska. Likewise, a legislation that provides a cheaper means of air transportation to the people of Alaska will be of no use to those in North Carolina. A legislation becomes useful only when it is directed at those who value it the most. Thus, it makes sense for the representatives of North Carolina and Alaska to support each other's legislation, if the passage of their legislation depends on their votes and will make the majority of their constituents happy.

Second, political exchange can be advantageous to representatives and voters because it permits groups to specialize in areas in which they have a comparative advantage. Exchange permits a

---

[1]Economists define the **marginal rate of substitution** as the amount of one good that is just sufficient to compensate the consumer--in our case, voter or representative--for the loss of a unit of the other good.

representative to become skilled in crafting legislation that will benefit his/her constituents, if s/he can count on the continued support of those constituents during elections. The constituents in turn will benefit from their votes, if they can count on their representative to promote legislation that are geared toward their interests.

Finally, voluntary political exchange makes possible for representatives to become more productive through cooperative efforts. Instead of engaging heavily on every policy, a representative can concentrate on those policies that are relatively more relevant to his/her constituents. Voluntary political exchange then allows representatives and voters to realize gains from the division of labor.

The motivating force behind political exchange is the pursuit of personal gain. Unless voters and representatives expect to gain from an exchange, it will not occur. Mutual gain forms the foundation for voluntary political exchange. Thus, political exchange is a positive-sum game.

As James Gwartney, Richard Stroup, and J. R. Clark (1985:437) remind us, the representative is a dynamic force in the democratic process. S/he seeks to offer voters an image and a bundle of political goods that will increase his/her chances of winning elections. The successful representative survives and may achieve private power, fame, and even fortune.

As such, Gwartney and his colleagues (1985:439) suggest that there is a strong incentive for the representative to stake out positions that will increase his/her vote total in the next election. A representative who refuses to give major consideration to gain votes increases the risk of being voted out of office and replaced by a more astute (and less public-minded) candidate. Competition in a democratic system forces even the most public-spirited representative to base his/her decisions primarily on political considerations.

Clearly, according to Gwartney and his partners, representatives often reap political gains by supporting special interest legislation, whether or not such legislation is inefficient. Since most voters lack the necessary information on a number of special interest issues, these authors suggest that representatives have a strong incentive to

(a) support views of a special interest group, (b) solicit from it both votes and money, (c) make the consequences of the special interest issue difficult for the average voter to understand (for example, by making the issue a part of a complex policy proposal), and (d) use funds obtained from the special interest group to promote their candidacy (Gwartney et al 1985:446).

Put differently, representatives have a strong incentive to solicit resources from special interest groups and use those resources to run not as a special interest candidate, but as the "people's candidate." Representatives who neglect this strategy run a greater risk of losing elections to those who accept such a reality of political life in a democratic society.

Indeed, a representative seeking to win an election has a strong incentive to exchange his/her vote for public sector action that yields substantial current benefits relative to costs. Thus, as Gwartney and his partners (1985:48) propose, public sector action tends to be biased in favor of legislation that offers immediate (and easily identified) current benefits at the expense of future costs that are difficult to identify. These authors also point out that there is often a bias against legislation that involves immediate and easily identifiable cost (for example, higher taxes) while yielding future benefits that are complex and difficult to identify. In essence, representatives tend to be shortsighted on issues whose future consequences are unclear. Nevertheless, with the various technological advancements in communications and information systems, recent developments have uncovered the collective ramifications of political and economic behavior.

Economists and political scientists have continually suggested that modern human beings have become agents and members of a global system. They have also produced much debate over what is being called the "New World Order." Governments have become more involved with each other's expanding political and economic transactions. People's needs are changing and so are their motivations. Therefore, the study of economic and political behavior is approached very differently now than it was just 15 or 20 years ago. Microchip technology has enabled the "information superhighway" to drastically change the way humans interact and the way humans make transactions.

In this context, there are many contributions to be derived from a discussion on *exchange structure*. It is essential to discuss exchange structure in order to understand how political behavior shapes political context and to account for shifts in global activity in terms of policy making. As expressed earlier, this chapter requires that considerable attention be given to discussing needs, motivations, interests, desires, etc., so that we may seriously outline and evaluate what is meant by exchange structure. Afterwards, by highlighting these factors somewhat differently than the way they are usually discussed (in economic and political theory), we can analyze global political behavior and context from the viewpoint of global exchange.[2]

Theoretical Underpinnings of Exchange Structure

Since our object of analysis in this chapter is *exchange structure* it is essential that we deal with some basic economic theoretical considerations of **exchange**, especially because political behavior and context in exchange structure stem from economic interests. In other words, what we are saying is that because agents engage in political behavior to gain access to and acquisition of resources to soothe their economic needs, our evaluation of exchange structures will employ some heavily borrowed methodological conclusions, insights, and limitations from economic theory in general. The borrowings are important for the promotion of: (1) a positivist approach to describing and defining actual sequences of events and outcomes in political processes; (2) a normative approach to deal with the predictive elements of expectations, i.e. of what ought to be gained from the processes of political exchange.

Usually, a discussion of exchange has the implied connection to a discussion of markets and goods. In general, exchange is usually perceived of in terms of trade or the trading sector of an economy and we usually speak of exchange as a "stock exchange" and a "foreign" or "international exchange" where goods are sold or traded, for example. Here, prices, costs, and values are in a process of being determined. From an economic and political standpoint, these things do exist in some concrete and measurable form, but there is also more to what we can refer to as exchange.

---

[2]Similar correspondence to a discussion of these factors can be found in economic theory. The question of methodology in economics has inspired considerable debate here as well.

If we allow for an economic approach to evaluating human behavior (which by no means is complete), it can be concluded that exchange is not simply a matter of markets, goods, and trade. Other human activities, such as marriage, have the implication that life for an agent is about making choices. These activities accumulate social costs. Humans desire preferences and choices and there are prices to be paid in exchange for having choices. So, exchange implies trade to the extent that trade means a type of trade-off or exchange of resources to satisfy desires.

In order to utilize this type of evaluation of exchange, it is important to further describe political behavior as the collectivity of motivations and actions which by various means shape and/or dictate the decisions of political actors, agents, and governmental institutions and set the expectations of activities of exchange. Therefore, we are saying that the behavior of voters, representatives, and states are all objects of political analysis. This is important in order to explain why entities behave in different ways at different levels. It will also allow us to understand how similar motivations inspire similar results.

Furthermore, it is also important to mention that neither do political entities simply fall from the sky nor do they exist in some form of complete isolation or degree of abstraction. Political scientists tend to assert that political behavior can be predicted with probable accuracy, i.e. because of maximizing tendencies or one's desire to acquire maximum benefits, political agents seek exchange to fulfill their best interests and acquire those objects which they desire (Gary Becker 1983). Their actions in terms of political behavior are predictable and, as the focus of study, is somewhat wedged between the Normative and Positive branches of Economics where it is suggested that exchange is both predictable and unpredictable. Regardless, exchange structure tells us some very interesting things about the way voters and representatives behave as well as how states and/or governments behave. Thus, four questions raise vital concerns to our understanding of exchange: (1) How is it that political agents negotiate and compromise to accomplish their goals? (2) What motivates them to act in one way or another? (3) What are the political and economic forces that promote or inhibit these actions? (4) Are exchange structures real?

An evaluation of political behavior and political context suggests that exchange structure is real in a general scientific sense. That is, real because it is qualifiable and quantifiable, and also real because it is existentially tied to various types of social environments and behaves in manners that can be observed and described. Thus, there are at least three attributes of economic theory that help us to appropriate the nature of exchange, following Becker (1983:109):

1. The allocation of material and immaterial goods to satisfy desires--where supply is dispersed to meet demand. The allocation and distribution of resource and wealth.

2. The market sector and market equilibrium--the existence of a medium of exchange where currency and credit are used to purchase goods. Constant flux of input and output. Equilibrium suggests a balance of payments. Supply meets demand and nullifies scarcity.

3. The allocation of scarce means to satisfy competing ends--production of wealth requires a labor force and not a shortage of manpower due to loss in population. Costs are means that should remain less or equivalent to the value of the end.

In a democratic state, political processes are characterized by the power of the vote. The voting process, in and of itself, is an expression of the will of the people; yet, to some degree, it is perceived as and taken completely for granted as a civic duty.[3] Voting allows members of the state to interact and become involved in political processes. Therefore, voter interaction has crucial importance. It is an instrument used by a politically informed public to weigh its support of the policies that are created by states and, more importantly, an instrument used by members of the public to centralize themselves in the creative process of policy-making. Thus, the way voters behave in relation to policies has serious implications for exchange. To understand the political behavior of voters and representatives in the context of exchange, and especially in terms of exchange with the state, it is necessary that we add a fourth and

---

[3]In a democratic state, voting is supposed to yield the will of the people. Through the expression of their civic duty, citizens become active participants in the political process. In exchange, the value of the vote has *exchangeable value.*

significant factor to our conception of exchange.

4. The function of the state as a policy-making machine--which erects policies that represent the best moral interests of its constituents.

Before we deal with the state's role as a policy-maker, we must first deal with those things which necessitate the existence of the state. Human beings, who are the major benefactors of the state and the mentors of the state, can be viewed as animals that make exchanges or animals who trade (John Creedy 1990:3). Creedy views man as an economizer, acting on the basis of self-interests and material gains. They are beings who seek alternatives to optimize desires. This does not mean that humans will always behave in manners which are always rational and promote their maximum benefit. Sometimes, access to information or the cost of transactions can prevent optimization (a thorough discussion of this aspect is presented in chapter six). There are also other non-economic variables which affect human behavior and attribute to instant changes in preferences and even ad hoc shifts in values. Therefore,

> human behavior is not compartmentalized, sometimes based on maximizing, sometimes not, sometimes motivated by stable preferences, sometimes by volatile ones, sometimes resulting in optimal accumulation of information, sometimes not. Rather, all human behavior can be viewed as involving participants who maximize their utility from a stable set of preferences and accumulate an optimal amount of information and other inputs in a variety of market (Becker 1983:199).

The activities of exchange require the existence of an established medium where it can occur. **Markets,** then, become the socially constructed and established media for exchange. The market is both a political and economic sector of society where agents collectively express their interests for exchange.

Voters and representatives have motivations, i.e. they have basic interests, needs, and desires, as was stated previously. Henry Odera Oruka (1987:467) suggests that these motivations can be collectively referred to as basic human needs. For example, the needs for food, clothing, and shelter are basic needs. There are also other needs/desires, like the desire for personal security and personal liberties, which must also be considered basic. Generally, the right of self-preservation and self-sustainability implies basic human needs. It may be concluded that self-preservation is guided by universal or "inherent" needs which all human beings rightfully deserve. These rights of physical security, health, and subsistence by necessity must be fulfilled, if a person is to be considered a full person and a member of the human family (a rational and moral agent). It follows then that a person cannot be expected to function rationally, unless s/he has access to a certain minimum which can be labelled a *basic human minimum* (Oruka 1987).

Exchange is the active process by which the basic minimum is acquired. It demonstrates how and what needs to be done in order to obtain desired ends. It is a compromise and most often a mutual arrangement, even though concerns about power relations suggest that it is not necessarily an amicable arrangement (a point that will be further discussed in relation to political accountability). Yet, the farmer who grows yams but needs clothing for his children and decides to barter or trade with the seamstress who needs yams and can trade or provide clothing is engaged in exchange. The relationship between these two agents is based on mutual reciprocity. In others words, because the two agents share mutual interests, exchange allows them to fulfill their desires by a simple transfer of goods or services.

It is mutual reciprocity that dictates political relations. However, in political processes, the only variation is that the exchangeable goods are slighted differently and have a more complex system of exchangeable value. The political relationships between voter and representative are mediated by the voting process which, by default, refers to the structures of exchange active in the state. The state itself is an issue of immense complexity.

The State

The state is a real political entity because of its responsibilities and civic requirements and maintains a right to self-preservation. Its self-preservation is justified because the state serves as the vehicle which provides and secures (through law and order) an absolute or basic human minimum for its citizens (Oruka 1987:4). The state, for example, is the only social agent which maintains legitimate authority to apply force as a measure to settle discrepancies. Nevertheless, this does not authorize the state to become an authoritarian regime. The people expect the state to remain democratic in exchange for their adherence and cooperation with its policies. Thus, as Richard Sandbrook suggests in his reference to reforms in Africa, shifting from authoritarianism to democracy requires these formal changes:

1. the official recognition of civil and political rights;

2. the legalization of opposition parties and of their right to organize support;

3. the organization of interest groups to protect their own interests, including those which were previously controlled or repressed;

4. the constitutional enshrinement of a set of democratic institutions and procedures, including laws governing elections, the independence of the judiciary, the role of the local government, and so on (Sandbrook 1993:91).

The structures of exchange in a political context allow the state to obtain access to a vastly increased flow of concessional resources. The voter demands that a large proportion of these resources, which are channelled through state agencies, be directed towards the achievement of major improvements in physical and social infrastructures, thus creating a framework for the expansion of public welfare and profitable private accumulation (Sandbrook 1993:22). Political value for voters and representatives translates as access to resources. Consequently, it appears that exchange structure is utilized by political agents to promote political agendas and self serving-interests. Nevertheless, the accepted rationalization is that exchange and voter participation serve as primary structures for rectifying, promoting, and guaranteeing human welfare; also, it justifies the existence of political exchange.

Ultimately, as suggested by David Easton (1965:358), the state serves as an instrument of policy. Constraints are placed on the state in its policy-making capacity.

Of course, it is possible to question the state's ability to implement its policies efficiently. The implementation of policy serves three basic objectives which a state performs as its duties and which voters expect from it.[4] These are:

1. The regulation of trade--the state is expected to be able to maintain and regulate the way goods and services are valued.

2. The rectification of social problems--the citizens expect the state agencies to address problems such as environmental issues or transportation or health issues.

3. The active promotion of the maxim of charity--the state is obliged to care for the needy by providing acceptable amounts of resources (Becker 1983).

The modern state, as the collective social representative by some means of government or organization, is also the provider of those things which are necessary to satisfy basic human needs. Through policy-making and regulation, the state provides individuals with degrees of access to material and immaterial goods, i.e. resources. In political terms, this is precisely what is meant by *exchange structure*. Policy-making establishes the avenues that political institutions utilize in order to provide its constituencies access to the accumulation of resources under its domain. It is also useful because it allows a state to create measures which will enforce its policy (Sandbrook 1993:23). At the highest social level, policy-making is a medium or, better yet, a reflection of trade and exchangeable values.

Voters and representatives are the constituents who seek political exchange and political trade. Again, by trade, we are implying a means to acquire primarily resources (or supplies) to meet needs (or demands). The voter trades his/her support for access to a secured portion of resources, while the representative trades his firm commitment to stand behind his campaign promises for the acquisition of political office. The representative also becomes the chief policy-making vehicle within the institutions and agencies of the state, although lobbyists and PACs (political action committees) are very prominent now and can play critical roles in policy and

---

[4]David Easton (1965) views the state primarily as a machine responsible for policy-making.

democratic reformation (see chapter three for more on this). The voter still depends on adequate policy-making from the representative so that the access and resources promised in campaigns are delivered.

In one sense, policy-making is the state's chief method of regulating the flux of resources under its domain. Yet, it serves as the primary method of protecting national security interests both on a domestic and international level. Therefore, the state is both an instrument of exchange as well as a suitor of exchange.

Exchange allows a state to preserve its national and territorial sovereignties. Whereas national sovereignty suggests a cultural identity, territorial sovereignty is based on a grouping of people into an organized state with a claim to a regional/territorial possession with control of the resources therein. States have an ethical obligation to enforce a domestic human minimum (Oruka 1987). Otherwise, disruption may occur when a state is incapable of providing for its citizens. Every state tarries over the issue of external interference. Inefficiency or flagrant abuse of power can translate into *coup d'état*.

Therefore, the desire of the state to be sovereign is also a factor in political exchange. States are forced to erect policies that promote positive *feedback* and protect themselves, given that territorial sovereignty is not an absolute right. Modern examples illustrate how external forces intervene in the domestic affairs of sovereign states in order to redistribute the wealth and resources of the inefficient states. This poses threats to the absolute right of a state's autonomy. In this manner, territorial sovereignty and supererogation are viewed as "prima facie" and not as absolute (Oruka 1987). However, the prerequisite of moral responsibility in the interests of global exchange suggests that self-preservation and national sovereignty are necessities in order to provide a human minimum. Thus, since the state is preoccupied with providing a standard basic human minimum, preserving its sovereignty and autonomy in controlling its internal affairs is absolute and/or a universal right.

Unfortunately, its ability to accomplish these objectives can be hindered by exchange and its policy-making. For the state, the activities of exchange are not as smooth in practice as they are conceptualized. As recent reports indicate, "Third World" states, for example, accumulated external debt totalling more than $1.32 trillion by 1993 (*World Bank Report* 1993). This demonstrates precisely why states are also in need of resources and also suitors of exchange.

States are coerced into accumulating a supply of resources for later usage.

The Structural Adjustment Programmes (SAPs) designed by international lending organizations have concluded that the main problem in debt repayment has been the role the state played in domestic policy-making in developing Third World economies. According to their logic, the problem was that governments dominated and become over-involved in the economic activities of their respective regions. It is believed that liberalized economies and privatizing state-run agencies would lead to sustainable growth and development. It is suggested then that these countries de-ideologize their economic institutions by creating free/open markets and placing less constraints on foreign investors. This critique has altered the way we perceive the role of the state in international economic exchange (Sandbrook 1993). Now, exchange has national and international implications for the modern state. For example, a labor problem in a Hershey's chocolate plant in the United States can affect cocoa prices in Ghana, and vice versa.

The state's role in exchange is based on moral responsibility. However, some have argued that international trade has been characterized by "unequal exchange," i.e. rich nations abusing poor nations by offering aid to poor countries as a means of bribing or paying them for favors that disguise their real interests in raw materials and access to markets. In international trade, poor and less developed countries are at a disadvantage and sometimes feel humiliated by global exchange. There is a severe problem at a higher level than in the way that states interact with each other. On a domestic level, states have a moral responsibility to aid the weak. Yet, on an international level, weak nations deal with the realization that they are compromising their territorial sovereignty by accepting aid from foreign sources and are thereby occasionally forced to make irrational decisions.

Voters have a similar complex. Once they have voted representatives into office, these representatives can ignore their campaign promises, further jeopardizing the stability of the state. Another major concern is that economic exchange is always fluctuating because of alterations in the market sector. These alterations can cause inflation and/or recessions. Political leadership can also vary. Thus, exchange structures are also affected by political and economic trends. Nevertheless, political leadership is supposed to match the demands of voters; here, accountability is significant and critical. It must also be stated that accountability is likewise a measure of how states are to interact with each other.

Global Exchange Structure and Accountability

There are three ways that we may approach accountability to understand its importance to exchange structure. First, we must understand that by accountability, we are referring to a system of operations which allows for the public to be informed and prepared to investigate and amend the characteristics and behavior of policy. Thus, accountability has three public features:

1. Voter accountability--where voters and the public are held accountable for their voting or nonvoting practices, i.e. as insiders and/or outsiders in political processes.

2. Representative accountability--where the political representatives are managing the agencies of the state for the best interests of all those under the jurisdiction of the state and not just in the interests of a selected few.

3. State accountability--accountability in terms of its interaction with its domestic affairs and its foreign affairs; i.e. the state's ability to promote a basic human minimum and global justice.

Accountability, as a standard for democratic states moving into the 21st century, will be primarily concerned with the division and distribution of the world's resources and wealth among the global population. Mainly, political agents hesitate to assume full responsibility for the maxim of political activities and very few take on the responsibilities of informing the public on debt crisis, health issues, environmental issues, etc. In most cases, a discussion of accountability leads us to various global problems that must be addressed. For example, the main problem which most developing states face is the problem of development. It has been said that money can buy influence. But for the recipients of World Bank and

IMF (International Monetary Fund) loans, money has bought underdevelopment. Authoritarian regimes have used aid to further strengthen their regimes and have expended resources to pay for extremely lavish lifestyles, leading to high levels of waste. This means that accountability may be better discussed in the negative as 'unaccountability.' Also, lending agencies practice policies that are now under intense scrutiny.

Political, economic, or even cultural exchange has been dictated by the Western powers (or superpowers as they like to call themselves). These powers are also not free from corruption themselves. The public in the West is demanding that its political representation be accountable for budgets and expenditures. Nevertheless, a shift is necessary to redirect exchange from the privileged position shared by the economic powers to isolated regions of the globe. As it is for states, the creation of global exchange policy cannot discriminate on the basis of race, sex., ethnicity, class, political affiliations or ideological alignment, nationality or religious orientation. This is also true on a domestic level. Voters must insist on an imperative that representatives remain ethically obligated to providing aid to the poor and have an unqualified moral duty to preserve humanity. Even if the humanity in question is outside the borders of the nation in question, voters must demand from their political representatives that they act morally in their relations with other states.

It may appear that we are promoting a justification for a welfare state; however, the state's compliance to this practice is the only way it can preserve its sovereignty. Remember that political behavior is motivated by the interests of its actors. The state's accountability is reflective upon the accountability of voters and representatives. Therefore, the promotion of social programs becomes a domestic ethical obligation to humanity for representatives, voters, and states. At the same time, it reinforces the right for a socially acceptable *basic human minimum* which can also be applied universally.

The promotion of global justice asserts that it is essential to call for the redistribution of the world's wealth, so that non-privileged groups may be provided with a share of the wealth for basic means of subsistence and also to directly confront the privileged status that some nations have gained in terms of the current process of distribution. Therefore, the idea of global exchange must remain deeply embedded in the concern for reparative redistribution of economic resources to address historical rectification and to effectively reverse the demarginalization of newly developing economies. In other words, the relationship that is characterized by *Dependency Theory*[5] characterizes the capitalist world system (D. K. Fieldhouse 1986:101). Capitalism was constructed mainly by Western Europe as it expanded its economic and political power from the sixteenth century onwards, culminating in the late-nineteenth and early twentieth-century colonial occupation of Africa and other continents (Walter Rodney 1972). In this system, Africa was cast in the role of consumer of Western manufactured exports.

Global exchange must be based on policies which can be enforced as standards of justice on an international level. Global justice must recognize the existence and rights of persons and states to self-preservation by ensuring that each state provides a basic human minimum. In this case, consideration needs to be applied to determine the impact of historical injustices suffered by underdeveloped countries. The impact of these injustices are important because they will help to demonstrate how the concept of a basic human minimum is also related to historical rectification as the result of the underdevelopment of "Third World" economies and Western economic aggrandizement. The question becomes whether or not states can be held accountable in terms of their interactions with other states. This is why we are hearing so much talk of treaties such as GATT (General Agreement on Trade and Tariffs) and NAFTA (North American Free Trade Agreement).

The world's resources and wealth do not belong to any particular group of human beings. Providing such a factor to de-legitimizing the ownership of the wealth gained as a result of colonial activities will serve as one of the ethical arguments to suggest replacing *foreign aid* with *foreign reparative redistribution*. From the previous result,

---

[5]**Dependency Theory** is rooted in specific economic and intellectual experiences of Latin American countries, particularly during the depression of the 1930s. Proponents of this theory postulate that underdeveloped countries have been exploited and dominated by the developed countries because the former had been subjugated, through colonialism and neocolonialism, to the dictates of the latter. Thus, economic development in the underdeveloped countries continues to be inimical to the dominant interests of the capitalists in developed countries.

exchange is not a matter of offering aid or charity, or even a matter of rectification. Exchange is directly related to the duty of correcting global underdevelopment, mainly because underdevelopment was a bitter fruit produced by colonialism. It displaced developing countries from their former natural historical courses of development during the colonial experience.

Based on exploitation and oppression, the West, through the establishment of mercantilist policies which became ultimately manifested in the capitalist mode of production, was able to strip those areas which it colonized of their resources and wealth. In the process, it forced them away from a natural progression of development which was demonstrable in their pre-colonial histories. It can be concluded then that colonialism underdeveloped what is referred to as the current underdeveloped nations of the world and is also further marginalizing them by maintaining hostile economic practices which continue to grant privilege status to Western countries. Rodney (1972) illustrates how Europe benefitted from African resources. His concept of "underdevelopment" illustrates the importance of relating an African perspective in any analysis. Rodney seems to be genuinely concerned with the way colonialism interrupted Africa's natural pattern towards development. As he puts it,

> All countries named as "underdeveloped" in the world are exploited by others; and the underdevelopment with which the world now is preoccupied is a product of capitalist, imperialist, and colonialist exploitation. African and Asian societies were developing independently until they were taken over directly or indirectly by the capitalist powers (Rodney 1972:14).

Rodney's analysis promotes the review of the possible impact that the considerable **loss of population** had on African society. Not only is he able to offer a brief exposition on how Europe managed to strip Africa of its **mineral wealth**, but he argues that in taking the most fit of African people to be sold in the **slave trade** also damaged and stunned Africa's ability to develop. Europe was able to cause a brain drain and a **labor shortage** in various African societies. Ghana went from being one of the richest and developed cultural centers in the world to a place depleted of its majesty in a matter of a few years. The impact of the slave trade on Africa was that it took all the artisans and craftsmen, leaving the weak behind. It also completely destroyed African forms of royalty and anything that resembled

African forms of social organization. In such a chaotic situation, the primary institutions necessary for progressive development deteriorated over a short period of time.

What makes Rodney's critique valuable is his demonstration of how Europe developed a sense of amnesia when it came to colonialism and the tremendous amounts of benefits it derived from its activities in Africa. Rodney, like W. E. B. Du Bois (1981), believed that the slave trade made **the accumulation of wealth** that Europe had acquired possible. In Rodney's words,

> The most spectacular feature in Europe which was connected with the African (slave) trade was the rise of seaport towns--notably Bristol, Liverpool, Nantes....Directly or indirectly connected to those ports there emerged the manufacturing centers which gave rise to the Industrial Revolution (Rodney 1972:101; parentheses are the authors').

Capital accumulation from the colonial policies financed the development of Europe. Africa, being raped by the colonial powers, shaped into mercantile states, and forced to become satellites for European interests, also lost its ability to sponsor fruitful growth.

The redistribution of wealth on an egalitarian basis addresses the unequal exchange that characterizes global economic activities. The destruction of African, Asian, and American states by their colonial agents allowed Europe to accumulate material wealth and to assert a hegemony and/or monopoly over the world's resources. Consequently, before these states can address the issue of economic readjustment and the possibility of humanitarian interference, an analysis of the impact of colonialism on the destruction of their developmental course takes priority.

Another important factor that needs to be emphasized in global exchange involves trading policies. For the most part, non-European states are being forced into becoming market centers for international trading interests. The disadvantage of late industrialization has made it possible for the West to export a vast amount of costly goods to developing countries. An inferior means of production at the domestic level means a costly waste of resources at the level of foreign exchange for those countries. Unfortunately, the policies of global exchange have meant that developing countries are almost totally dependent on external exchange as a means of survival. It also means that the security and stability of developing states fluctuates with international trends. Therefore, if a major international trading partner wishes to cut and reduce economic relations with a particular state, it would have devastating effects on that economy.

The international lending institutions have demonstrated the same ideological bias and destructive approach in their attitudes toward lending money to developing countries (Sandbrook 1993). Privatizing and liberalizing economic institutions mean that foreign domination becomes unavoidable, since foreign investors are the only actors that maintain the ability to produce capital for investment and also control the rights to mine and produce raw materials worldwide.

Multinational corporations (MNCs) have total control over the raw materials and minerals. Obviously, this is because the capital requirements necessary to exploit these raw materials are extremely high. As a result, all activities, including exploration and production, are still in the hands of foreign companies (Fidelis Akagha 1992:9).

Developing countries may want to reconsider their exposure to international finance, which would allow them to question whether or not their autonomy and control of resources is necessarily worth forsaking for Western-style development. It is difficult because developing states are extremely dependent on external finance for their economic survival. This means that it is unlikely, given the present state of the global economy, that self-sufficient development in those countries will occur in the near future. Overall, the evaluation of global exchange trends reveal that there is much room for moral reform. The developing states exist as objects of neo-colonial interests and are the victims of current international exchange structures, serving the interests of global colonizers. The humiliation of unequal exchange is incomparable to the realization of having fallen prey to a third form of colonialism.

George Shepherd has insisted that the United Nations

> proclaim a jubilee year of debt forgiveness, together with a renewed commitment to self-reliance and developmental rights. The 50th anniversary of the Universal Declaration of Human Rights in 1955 would be an appropriate time for such a reconciliation of North-South Conflict. Debt forgiveness is essential if the new democratic initiatives are to succeed. Moreover, a very practical basis for debt cancellation between North and South could be the proclamation of new trade agreements based on equity and sustainability (1990:1).

Foreign aid should ascend to the level of reparative redistribution of the world's economic resources and wealth. The developed countries of the world have, without doubt, forcibly accumulated more than their rightful share of global resources and wealth from benefits directly or indirectly derived from injustices committed in the so-called "Third World." In the interests of global exchange, the only reasonable course of action must include the United Nations' willingness to enact policies that foster historical rectification. If the United Nations can effectively promote a solution on the basis of reparative redistribution, it could possible deal with these worldwide problems:

1. global conflict;

2. the regulation of the activities of MNCs and lending institutions in the "Third World" as a method of dealing with the debt crisis;

3. the promotion of policies that adjust the damage caused by severe historical experience; and finally

4. serving as a mechanism to deal with international corruption and abuse in order to help struggling governments to stabilize themselves.

However, as Sandbrook reminds us,

> It would be naive to treat the strategy's main proponents, the World Bank and IMF, as non-ideological agencies open ended searching for cures for Africa's financial disequilibria, stagnation, poverty, and oppression. The geopolitical interests of the Western powers and (where these differ) the needs of the internationalized capital will inevitably influence revisions in the dominant development ideology. Since their creation, The IMF and the World Bank have consistently aimed to integrate as many national economies as possible into a multilateral global capitalist economy (Sandbrook 1993:4).

Indeed, global political accountability is made difficult by international agencies, such as the World Bank and IMF, whose multilateral mismanagement lay in economic analysis more derivative from ideology than sound theory. In this ideology, the relative exchanges, which provide such insights, are carried to their *reductio ad absurdum*.

Conclusion

We have attempted in this chapter to discuss *exchange structure* in more than a general economic sense, because this was necessary to show how political behavior in exchange structure stems from the sequential needs and wants of voters and representatives. We have also attempted to show how shifts in technology, especially in communicative technology, has meant that political behavior has global ramifications. It is expected then that political processes and institutions will continue to look more global in perspective, as we have seen with recent developments in global structures. Expanding the United Nations Security Council (UNSC) could mean that the debt crisis in the developing world would finally be addressed. A nation like Nigeria has a great amount of potential and could use its presence in the United Nations General Assembly (UNGA) to lobby for other developing countries. The issue of past injustices could also take precedence. It appears impossible for African states to pay back developmental loans, especially at such high interest rates. The liberalization of African economies will only benefit Western companies because they are the only ones with the capital to take advantage of the reforms. Africa will be at the mercy of the MNCs like it was at the mercy of colonialists.

Reparative redistribution appears as the only salvation for "Third World" states. However, this should not overlook the responsibility and accountability of those who plan to take leadership roles in these societies. The United Nations, through the regulation of economic forces in the "Third World," could serve as a mechanism that would guarantee that states provide a basic human minimum. It could also regulate the activities of MNCs and NGOs (non-governmental agencies) to verify that they are agents of development and not agents of devastation. If the United Nations is able to restructure itself, it is possible for it to serve a desperately needed role in post-Cold War international relations. The structure of global exchange requires this sort of transitions as people's needs and interests become more and more common across the globe.

Chapter 3

Action Structure

Introduction

As we mentioned in chapter one, **action structure**, as used in this book, comprises the acts of *voting* and *representing*. The term 'structure' is employed here for the same reason that it was used in discussing **exchange structure** (refer to chapter two)--to direct attention to orders of occurrence and to the decision procedures through which such orders emerge. Thus, the actions of voting and representing occur in constrained linear sequences: they are not randomly ordered; there is a pattern and predictability to their occurrences. Furthermore, the acts of voting and representing are situated in political participation (for more on this, refer to chapter five), such that what counts as a particular action is strongly constrained by what action precedes, what action is intended, what action is intended to follow, and what action actually does follow. The action structure is therefore critical in fulfilling the ritual constraints of political behavior; that is, the interpersonal requirements of a democratic polity.

Before delving into the discussion of the acts of voting and representing, however, we will begin by discussing some theoretical notions about the concept of *action*. This is important because voting and representing are displays of affected behavior; and in order to understand these actions, it makes sense to examine some of the reasons that propel people to perform these acts voluntarily.

Max Weber (1947) provides a typology of four types of action in terms of the arrangement of its inner conscious components. His action types are as follows: (1) *Zwekrational* ("rationally purposeful") is an action addressed to a situation with a plurality of means and ends in which the actor is free to choose his/her means purely in terms of efficiency; (2) *Wertrational* ("rational in terms of values") is action in which the means are chosen for their efficiency, but the ends are fixed in advance; (3) *Affective* is when emotional factors determine the means and ends of action; (4) *Traditional* action is when both means and ends are fixed by custom.

Weber's action typology is very important because it underscores the nominalistic perspective: i.e. only individuals and individual actions exist. Consequently, only individual acts exist; no new super-individual entities exist. A *way* of acting is thus not a new *thing*.

Talcott Parsons' (1937/1949) starting point for the modern theory of action is the idea of the intrinsic rationality of action. For him, action consists of "ends," "means," and "conditions." Thus, according to him, rationality of action hinges on a scientific determinable relation of means to the conditions of the situation. Parsons further argues that two positivistic positions--a rationalistic and an anti-rationalistic--tended to alter the place of rationality in action. The former made obsolete the distinction between ends, means, and conditions of action, making it a process of adaptation to the situation. The latter eliminated rationality altogether.

In a later work, Parsons (1951) treats action itself as a system: a plurality of interacting persons "motivated in terms of a tendency to the 'optimization of gratification' and whose relation to their situations, including each other, is defined and mediated in terms of a system of culturally structured and shared symbols" (pp.5-6). For Parsons, the action system of the individual has two basic aspects: gratificational and orientational. He calls the former "cathectic" and the latter, "cognitive." Parsons perceives human action to display both desires and ideas. The objects that may satisfy needs are many; for example, there are numerous items that can satisfy hunger. He suggests, therefore, that "cognitive mapping has alternatives of judgement or interpretation as to what objects are or what they 'mean.' There must be ordered selection among such alternatives. The term 'evaluation' will be given to this process of ordered selection" (p.7). Stated differently, action is to be analyzed into ideas, desires, norms or values.

In addition, Parsons maintains that an action system brings motivational and symbolic elements into an ordered system. This order is normative and can be either intrinsic or instrumental. Norms are critical to *roles*, and roles organize the expectations of the individual in relation to a particular interaction context and govern interaction with one or more "alters" in complimentary roles. Roles are also critical to *institutions*, which are role integrates of strategic structural significance in the social system (1951:40-45).

Furthermore, Parsons suggests that in any given action, the actor strives for optimum gratification. He notes, however, that in order for an action system to be organized or integrated, some gratifications must be renunciated. An individual cannot want everything; s/he has to be neutral about some things. Parsons goes on to propose four postulates. The first is that "the polarity of affectivity-neutrality formulates the patterning out of action with respect to this basic alternative." The second is that the individual is confronted with a choice of pursuing his/her own private interests ("self-orientation") and those s/he shares with others ("collectivity-orientation"). The third is that the action may be determined either by feelings or ideas. "The primacy of cognitive values then may be said to imply a *universalistic* standard of role-expectation, while the appreciative values implies a *particularistic* standard". Moreover, in a given action, alternatives exist in terms of the properties of social objects. "With respect to characteristics of the object it is that of the focus on its qualities or attributes as distinguished from focus on its performance" that is the "one dilemma which is of the most generalized significance." Put differently, an individual may value another individual to the social action on the basis of what the latter is (ascription) or what s/he does (achievement). The final one is that another action alternative is that which defines the scope of ego's interest in the object. One possibility is that the actor can define the role "as orienting to the social object in *specific* terms" as opposed to orientation in a "*diffuse*" mode (1951:60-66). With this discussion of *action* serving as a guide, we can now examine the acts of voting and representing with a relatively keener sense of their theoretical implications.

Voting

Derived from the Latin word *votum* ('vow' or 'wish'), voting is commonly defined as a formal act of expressing an opinion, preference, or will in response to a proposed decision. Thus, E. E. Schattschneider (1960:103) is quite correct when he states that "Voting is not an isolated social phenomenon; it is a part of the social condition of the people." In examining the available literature on voting, two interrelated themes tend to recur. These are: (1) voting preference or logic of choice, and (2) voting behavior. Each of these themes is discussed separately.

Voting Preference or Logic of Choice

Although having the power to vote is a *sine qua non* of any democratic society, to exercise that power poses a dilemma in choice, especially for the voter who wishes to make a rational choice. As William Mitchell (1974:33) insists, not to recognize the inherent dilemma confronting a voter who, approaching the polls for the first time, wants to do good for him-/her-self, his/her generation, and the nation, would be quite foolish.

Conventional voting studies by political scientists, Mitchell points out,

> tell us that most voters are (1) not well informed, (2) apathetic if not cynical, (3) inclined to vote as their parents did, (4) inclined to vote as members of their social groupings previously have, and (5) inclined to be somewhat less than rational in their decision processes and their choices (1974:33).

Mitchell (1974:33) also argues that although highly impressive and persuasive evidence exists to support the first four propositions, voters need not behave this way. Thus, he suggests that the rational voter must ask him-/her-self the following four questions, if s/he wants the decision process well within his/her grasp: (1) Is voting worthwhile? (2) Can my vote influence the electoral outcome? (3) What are the "costs" of voting? (4) Can I influence public policy? (Mitchell 1971). The ultimate question then is: What factors shape voting choice or preference?

Two studies of American presidential elections in the 1940s by Paul Lazarsfeld, Bernard Berelson, and Hazel Gaudet (1944), and Bernard Berelson, Paul Lazarsfeld, and William McPhee (1954) indicate that *social group membership* and *social status* were good determinants of a voter's choice or preference. But as Richard Watson (1984:85-86) demonstrates, group affiliation has not meant as much in predicting a voter's choice in recent voting as it once did.

According to Robert Cord and his colleagues (1985:225-226), in democratic nations such as the United States, where class divisions are tentative, and Western Europe, where the traditional stratification of social classes is pervasive, perhaps the most important determinant of a voter's party identification is social-class membership. Social class is the single most pervasive influence on a voter's political outlook. Generally, blue-collar industrial workers are more likely to vote for the party at the left of the political spectrum, whereas members of the middle and upper classes tend to have relatively more conservative political leanings.

The question that emerges then is: How can an analyst tell when a lot of class voting is taking place? Robert Alford (1963) has devised an "index of class voting"[6] as a more objective measure of class voting cross-nationally or across time. In examining the election results of four Anglo-American countries from 1952 to 1962, Alford derived the following indices: Australia 33, Canada 8, Great Britain 40, and the United States 16. In other words, class voting was much stronger in Australia and Great Britain than in Canada and the United States.

A major study of American presidential elections in the 1950s by Angus Campbell et al (1964) reveals that the single most important determinant of voting at that time was the voter's *party affiliation*. Philip Converse (1976:34) calls this period the "Steady State" period, as the average voter looked to the party label of the candidates to guide him/her on how to cast his/her vote amid the complexity of personalities, issues, and events. However, Watson (1984:83-84) points out that partisan affiliation began to change in the mid-to-late 1960s in the United States. He adds that it is difficult to pinpoint the particular reasons for the decline in partisanship among American

---

[6]The "index of class voting" = % of manual workers voting for the "left" party - % of non-manual workers voting for that party.

voters. One factor Watson suspects for this decline is the decreased transfer of partisanship from one generation to another.

As Leon Epstein (1976:78-85) reveals, party identification influences European voters differently compared to the way it does American voters because it means different things in Europe and in the United States. The reason for this, according to him, is that Americans, although are registered with a party, cannot be counted on to vote according to their party registration, whereas Europeans, few of whom are party members, are more likely to vote according to their party memberships.

Campbell and his associates (1964) also suggest that as a matter of logic, *issues* are potentially important in determining how a voter casts his/her ballot under three conditions: (1) the voter must be aware that an issue or a number of issues exists, (2) the issues must be of some personal concern to the voter, and (3) the voter must perceive that one party better represents his/her own thinking on the issues than the competing party(ies). However, when Campbell and his colleagues applied these three conditions to the American voters in the 1952 and 1956 elections, their findings suggested that relatively few voters met these criteria.

Relatively recent studies by Gerald Pomper (1975) and Norman Nie, Sydney Verba, and John Petrocik (1976) find that there is a rise in the potential for voting on the basis of issues. Watson's (1984:90) analysis also supports the view of the voter moving away from conceiving of politics primarily from the vantage point of group benefits and towards looking at politics in broader terms of issues and general political ideas.

A good example of the importance of issues in shaping voting preference is the case of William Jennings Bryan. In 1990, Bryan based his candidacy on a single issue: a "Populist" call for a silver standard for the American dollar. He identified himself so strongly with the issue that even today the mention of his name yields the response "cross of gold." Although he lost the election, Bryan's case illustrates an election where one issue dominated voter decisions (Cord et al 1985:230).

A corollary to the role of issues in determining voting choice pointed out by Converse (1964) is *political ideology*: the increased ability of the voter to be able to relate political issues to one or another on the basis of a general liberal-conservative continuum. A relatively recent study by Arthur Miller (1981) also demonstrates the importance of political ideology in determining voting preferences by showing that many persons voted for Ronald Reagan in 1980 because they agreed with his conservative policies.

As Robert Cord and his associates (1985:225-226) suggest, just as some people are more likely to vote than other groups, so are some people more likely to be "liberal" than others. According to them, young people are more likely to vote for the liberal parties, whereas the older people are more likely to vote for conservative parties.

Warren Miller and Teresa Levitin's study (1976) reveals that the *candidates' influence* has an effect on voting preference. They also note that the difficulty involved in determining a particular candidate's influence on such a choice can be made much easier by focusing on the specific qualities of that candidate. Also, as Watson (1984:87-88) maintains,

> Voter's (sic) attitudes on candidates stem from numerous sources, including the associations voters make between candidates and their partisan affiliations, candidates' stands on issues, voters' perceptions on how candidates have managed or would manage the government, and candidates' personal qualities such as background and experience, personality and character traits, personal and political "style," and competence and trustworthiness.

As Cord and his colleagues (1985:231) maintain, although a candidate's influence is seldom the sole reason for voting preference, it is sometimes very important in determining an election. They cite the cases of Charles de Gaulle of France, Pierre Elliott Trudeau of Canada, Willy Brandt of Germany, and John F. Kennedy of the United States as some of the more charismatic political figures of recent times whose influences determined key elections. Cord and his colleagues also note that televised election campaigns have heightened candidates' influence throughout the world (see also chapter six for a discussion on the important role of television in modern democracies).

The preceding discussion reveals that the reasons which prompt an individual to vote and influence others to remain at home on election day are varied. In other words, voting preference or logic of choice is influenced by many factors: social group membership, social status, party affiliation, issues, ideology, and candidates' influence.

The magnitude of each factor seems to change over time.

Voting Behavior

As Herbert Winter and Thomas Bellows (1985:244) show, the significance of voting varies with the importance of elections in determining winning candidates. Consequently, some former Communist states, such as Albania, report voter turnouts of 100 percent, and typical turnouts in former Communist countries were almost invariably in the 95 percent-plus range. While, on the one hand, many Western countries report turnouts in excess of 80 percent, on the other hand, United States congressional elections in non-presidential election years draw between 30.1 percent and 46.1 percent during the past six decades.

Thus, the curious observer must ask why there is such profound variation among different countries and within the same country. The answer to this question hinges on examining the determinants of voting behavior. Consequently, in order to delineate these determinants, one must investigate two major questions: (1) Why do some people vote? (2) Why do some people fail to vote?

1. Why Some People Vote

Characteristics such as ethnicity, age, income level and education (or class), gender, and area of residence are major determinants of why some people vote. What follows is an examination of each of these determinants.

Ethnicity. In the United States, for example, not many decades ago there was a marked difference in the voting patterns of African-Americans and European-Americans; African-American voting rates were much lower. A great deal of this has changed as income and education levels of African-Americans have risen. Also, the Voting Rights Act of 1965 helped in lowering the barriers placed in the way of African-American registration, especially in the South. To encourage African-Americans to register and vote in 1984, the Rev. Jesse Jackson campaign doggedly for the Democratic nomination, even though he knew he had no chance of winning. Now, nationwide

African-American turnout is closer to that for European-Americans. Of particular importance in this development is the fact that African-Americans have learned the value of their votes. Many racist European-American politicians got the message and have become respectful toward their African-American constituents. Chicanos have quickly learned to register and vote (Cord et al, 1985:221).

During the first electoral participation by immigrants[7] in the 1976 Swedish local and regional elections, only 58.8 percent of the immigrants entitled to vote, compared to 91.7 percent of the native Swedish electorate, voted. In other words, one-third of the immigrant electorate stayed at home. Limited voting rights and tremendous information problems accounted for the low turnout. However, in the southern region, which had a larger proportion of non-Nordic immigrants, there was a slightly higher turnout. In essence, contrary to expectation, Finns, Norwegians, and Danes were less assiduous voters than southern Europeans (Tomas Hammar 1977:3).

Age. Young people under the age of 25 typically feel less politically involved compared to those who are older. Consequently, young people tend to vote less. By 1985, about half of the American citizens 18 to 25 years of age, for example, had not registered to vote (Cord et al 1985:221).

In 1971, the Twenty-Sixth Amendment to the United States Constitution lowered the American voting age from 21 to 18. At almost the same time, most other democracies did the same. In all these countries, the results were similar to that of the United States: the newly enfranchised young people did not vote as much as their elders (Cord et al 1985:221).

Income Level and Education (or Class). In the United States, citizens with large incomes are more likely to vote than those who are less affluent. Also, citizens who are well educated are more likely to vote than those who dropped out of secondary or high school. Even though certain voters often combine the two characteristics (i.e. higher education makes it possible to earn a large income), the two influence voting in different ways. The former has to do with having a stake in election outcomes; the latter has to do with the broader question of interest and sophistication (Cord et al 1985:220).

---

[7]These immigrants were mostly Yugoslavs, Turkish, Polish, and Finnish.

In European democracies, where class-based political parties are the norm and actively encourage citizens to vote, smaller differences exist in participation rates between classes than in the United States. In general, strong identification with a political party or candidate tends to encourage citizens to vote (Winter and Bellows 1985:248).

Gender. In the past, males were more likely to vote than females in almost every Western society. This was due, in large part, to the fact that females had only comparatively recently won the right to vote in these societies. In Switzerland, for example, it was not until 1971 that females were enfranchised. Since 1920, when female suffrage was granted in the United States after a great deal of struggle by women, the gap between male and female voter turnouts has been narrowing precipitously (Cord et al 1985:222).

Area of Residence. In most democracies, the fact that citizens living in urban areas tend to vote more than those living in rural areas is hardly surprising. This reflects the easier accessibility of voting booths in the urban areas, where a relatively smaller area (as in New York City) can comprise a voting district with the same population as a rural district of several square miles (as in Alaska). However, unlike those in Great Britain and the United States, rural areas in France traditionally turn out a higher percentage of voters than do urban areas. This is due to the fact that in France, local politics in small towns is conducted on a much more intimate level than the depersonalized politics of the large urban areas (Cord et al 1985:222).

Citizens who reside in the same community for a long time are more likely to vote than are transients or newcomers. This is because long-term residents of any community feel more connected to their neighborhoods, and are thus more likely to participate in groups and activities that will strengthen that community (Cord et al 1985:222).

2. Why Some People Fail to Vote

As Schattschneider (1975:95-96) observes, the distinction between citizens who vote and those who do not deserves to be examined because it may be the most important aspect in a democracy. The most striking fact about this phenomenon, according to him, is that with some important exceptions, non-voting seems to be voluntary. Thus, the ultimate question is the following: Why do some people fail to vote?

For Schattschneider (1975:107), the root of the problem of non-voting hinges on (a) the way in which alternatives are defined, (b) the scale of competition and organization, and (c) the issues that are developed. The fact that a large non-voting population exists in the United States, he maintains, provides an insight into the nature of the unresolved historic tensions in the political system itself.

Winter and Bellows (1985) mention a number of other factors that may lead some people not to vote. Some people see voting as threatening to their relations with family members and friends. Others may perceive voting as a futile exercise due to a sense of personal inadequacy, a feeling that political forces cannot be managed, or that a large gap exists between democratic ideals and political reality. Some people may simply be satisfied with their political system and see no reason to vote. Others who believe that no effective choice exists between candidates or parties may choose not to vote. Bad weather or a belief that one's candidate or party will lose (or win) may keep some voters at home on election day. Some voters may decide not to vote simply because an election is held on a normal work day (pp. 248-249).

According to Anthony Downs (1957:260-261), for every rational individual, if the costs of voting outweigh the returns, s/he will abstain from voting. Downs also offers a number of propositions for "rational abstention" which can be paraphrased as follows:

1. When voting is costless, every citizen who is indifferent abstains.

2. If voting is costly, it is rational for some citizens with preferences to abstain.

3. The cost of information acts in effect to disenfranchise low-income groups relative to high-income groups when voting is costly.

4. Voting costs may also disenfranchise low-income citizens relative to wealthier citizens.

It is apparent that Downs' approach for analyzing non-voting behavior differs from those conventionally used by other political analysts. He emphasizes a concept of voting behavior based on rational calculation of self-interest.

Representing

As used in this book, *representing* refers to serving in a political system by delegated authority. As such, a *representative* is an individual who acts for or on behalf of other citizens in the decision-making process. *Representation,* then, is an outcome in the conditions that make it possible for some members of a society to act for the society as a whole. Following Roderick Bell and David Edwards (1974), a distinction can be made between "external" and "internal" representation, which they define as follows:

> *External representation* indicates the political society seen from without. We might know very little about the internal organization of a country--the People's Republic of China, for a good example--and yet find that country effectively and undeniably represented as an existing, viable political society....*Internal representation* is the political society experienced from within. The articulated institutions of a society--president, king, parliament--and the consequent relations among its members constitute the common framework within which reality is perceived by individuals in the society....(pp.5-6).

Consequently, the articulation of any democratic society naturally involves many political struggles between those citizens who seek to represent their fellows. To understand these political struggles, the following discussion on the notion of *representing* is divided into two major categories: (1) theories of representation, and (2) types of representation.

Theories of Representation

Winter and Bellows (1985:227-235) and Cord and his associates (1985:236-240) have provided excellent summaries of classical and contemporary theories of representation. These theories range from the allocation of all popular authority to the sovereign, to rule by the "general will" with direct popular participation or of indirect representation. The discussion that follows is based to a great extent on these scholars' works. Other scholars' views on the issues are also included where appropriate.

1. Classical Theories of Representation

Hobbesian Theory of Representation. Thomas Hobbes' (1588-1679) response to the question why people form governments was that without such an instrument, no one could be secure from attack. To protect themselves, people long ago formed governments, renounced their personal independence, and formed a "social contract" that authorized the sovereign to establish laws that would protect every citizen equally. For Hobbes, government was founded on "consent of the governed," with one exception: Once authority is given to the sovereign, it cannot be taken back. Even if the sovereign were to become a tyrant, the people cannot trade him/her in. Witnessing the English civil wars, Hobbes wrote that anarchy (the state of nature), where everyone is free to do as s/he pleases, is infinitely worse than even the most despotic ruler (Cord et al 1985:236, Winter and Bellows 1985:228).

Lockian Theory of Representation. John Locke (1632-1704) modified Hobbes' view by proposing that rulers must be responsible to the governed. For Locke, the social contract binds the government and the people to a set of responsibilities: citizens must obey the government only if it honors its obligation to protect them. The people have the right to replace the government, if the government violates the trust (Cord et al 1985:236).

Rousseaunian Theory of Representation. Jean-Jacques Rousseau's (1712-1778) view differed from those of Hobbes and Locke. Rousseau argued that representation went hand-in-hand with inequality and loss of freedom. He believed that humans are intelligent, rational beings and are quite capable of making their own decisions. Thus, for Rousseau, the ideal is a city-state, where every citizen can participate in deliberative assemblies of government. Representation, according to him, was tyranny, unless the representatives only conveyed the desires of the people. Representatives are to transmit decisions, nothing more (Cord et al 1985:236, Winter and Bellows 1985:230).

In sum, the views of Hobbes, Locke, and Rousseau represent a range of theories--from the allocation of all popular authority to the sovereign to rule by the "general will" with direct popular participation. Since these three philosophers were writing about events covering the 1500s-1700s, the question here then is the following: What theories exist about contemporary representation?

2. Contemporary Theories of Representation

In examining discussions about contemporary representation, two issues seem to recur. The first issue is about the obligation representatives have to the people who elect them. The second issue deals with how much control voters should have over the representatives they elect. In addressing these issues, the following theories of contemporary representation have been offered.

Symbolic Theory of Representation. This refers to a situation where the head of state is the "symbol" of that state: s/he represents the citizens by "standing for" them. In Great Britain, for example, Queen Elizabeth II is said to "stand for" the people, and her lifestyle reflects the traditional power and glory of the country. However, very few people today would be content to elect a representative to office solely on the grounds that s/he symbolizes the national or local character. Voters are now more concerned with how a representative will act on their behalf once in office (Cord et al 1985:237).

Constituent Theory of Representation. In this type of representation, when a representative is elected from a particular constituency, his/her responsibility is to vote for all bills that will help that constituency, even though some of those bills may work to the disadvantage of the rest of the country. The issue that emerges in terms of this type of representation is whether or not representatives should vote according to conscience, even when it means going against constituents' wishes (Cord et al 1985:237).

One answer to this dilemma was offered by Edmund Burke (1729-1797) who argued that whereas a representative must act on the behalf of his/her constituents, s/he is not bound to act as they would wish at all times. He believed that a representative ought to represent the entire country, not just his/her constituency.[8] According to Burke, this idea did not violate the principles of representative government, because if the citizens do not like the way their representative acts,

---

[8] Edmund Burke himself was a member of the British parliament and felt that he represented the entire British Empire, not just his district of Bristol (Cord et al 1985:237).

they can vote him/her out of office at the subsequent election (Winter and Bellows 1985:228, Cord et al 1985:237-238).

The counter argument to that of Burke is that a representative is elected to act for his/her constituents and s/he must act as they want him/her to act, even if it means going against his/her better judgment. The major problem with this theory of "re-presentation" is the difficulty in finding out what constituents want so that the representative can carry out their wishes. In the United States, for instance, the average congressperson represents nearly half a million citizens, and the likelihood that s/he will speak to or receive mail from even five percent of that number is slim, even on major issues. This problem is compounded by the fact that there is always a wide range of public opinion on any issue (Cord et al 1985:238).

Correspondence Theory of Representation. This theory emerged in response to the fact that even if a representative were able to act as the voice of his/her constituency, s/he could easily be accused of being unrepresentative on other grounds. This is because most representatives are not at all representative in reflecting the social makeup of their districts. For the most part, representatives are middle- or upper-class professionals, often lawyers, overwhelmingly male, generally older than their constituents, and much better educated. In the United States legislature, for example, WASPS (white Anglo-Saxon Protestants) dominate (Cord et al 1985:238).

Some observers have suggested that the answer to this problem lies in having a representative government that corresponds to the characteristics of the general public. In the case of the United States, for instance, since 53 percent of the population is female, these observers insist that its legislative bodies must be 53 percent female. The proposed government must also have African-Americans, Roman Catholics, Jews, etc. in proportion to their numbers in the population (Cord et al 1985:239).

Functional Theory of Representation. The idea of functional representation is an attempt to resolve the inevitable dilemma of the correspondence approach of representation. The tenor of the functional notion of representation is that the legislature be structured around the major social or economic interests in a country: agriculture, organized labor, industry, the arts and sciences, etc. instead of geographical districts. Each interest would then be assigned seats according to its relative size and importance to the economy, and citizens would vote not as individuals, but as businesspersons, laborers, or farmers, etc (Cord et al 1985:239-240).

The functional approach of representation is used in the Irish Seanad (Senate). Of its sixty members, eleven are chosen by the prime minister and six by the universities, and the remaining forty-three are elected by the national legislature and county borough councils from lists of candidates generated by five vocational panels. These panels are shaped according to occupational categories whose choices represent cultural, educational, agricultural, labor, industrial, and commercial interests. However, the Irish Seanad is partly a ceremonial upper house with very little power (Cord et al 1985:240).

Also, as Charles Anderson, Fred Mehden, and Crawford Young (1967:77) point out, the functional approach has been used as the most widespread and effective formula for coming to terms with diversity in a number of countries. This has been called the "balanced ticket" in ethnically conscious areas of the United States, especially New York and New England, or what has been termed "ethnic arithmetic" in West Africa. In such cases, efforts are made to distribute the visible leadership functions within the state in some rough proportion to the strength and self-consciousness of the primary cultural groups within the polity. Anderson and his colleagues cite Lebanon as probably the most extreme case: The President is, by institutionalized tradition, a Maronite Christian, the Prime Minister is a Sunni Muslim, and the chairman of Parliament is a Shi'ite. For many years before the bloody and protracted Lebanese civil war, this arrangement allowed primary groups to have a psychic assurance that their communal interests were being defended, that there would be no risk of the state being converted into an engine of hegemony of one cultural group over another.

Types of Representation

Similar to Charles Andrain's (1983:178-181) approach in comparing the structural dimensions of state power, rather than describe types of representation according to formal government institutions (for example, presidency, cabinet, parliament, courts of law, etc.), we base our descriptions on general structural dimensions that reflect interactions among the central state organs, lower government agencies, and social groups. As such, we identify five types of representation. These are discussed separately.

1. Monopolistic Representation

This type of representation refers to the case of a powerful representative who monopolizes the decision-making process, denying lower government agencies and social groups the right to make policies. The monopolistic representative uses the military and police as agents of physical coercion to wield crucial control. Monopolistic representatives tend to prevail at the early stage of a country's development. As Andrain (1983:181) points out, in Europe between 1600 and 1800, "absolute monarchs" ruled states as France, Prussian Germany, Spain, and Russia. In France, for example, Louis XIV (1643-1715) declared himself the "Sun King," i.e. the radiating center of all political authority. Claiming to embody the state, Louis XIV proclaimed: "L'État, c'est Moi" (I am the state). Andrain also points out that similarly, after African territories gained political independence from their European colonizers during the late 1950s and early 1960s, monopolistic rule became widespread. Although colonial rule had destroyed the traditional monarchies, new presidential monarchies emerged, led by military officials or nationalist politicians (this point is highlighted in the preceding chapter).

2. Centralized Representation

This type of representation exists when representatives in the national government gain dominance over representatives of local political units, such as village assemblies, town councils, municipal governments, and provincial administrations. The centralized approach allows those representatives in the national government to maintain the territorial integrity of the country. As Winter and Bellows (1985:235) remind us, centralized representation existed in the former Soviet Union and the Eastern European bloc. In the former Soviet Union, for instance, although the Constitution vested all powers in the elected "Supreme Soviet," effective power rested with the Communist party which controlled both the government and nomination to local and Supreme Soviets. Similar types of representation exist today in Cuba and the People's Republic of China, to name a few.

3. Coordinated Representation

Coordinated representation refers to a situation where representatives of a single agency formally orchestrate the functional activities of government. According to Andrain (1983:179), in many Western societies, for example, the monarch originally claimed to exercise "sovereignty," i.e. the absolute legal right to make final decisions binding on the society. S/he and the royal bureaucracy coordinated central government activities. When the monarch lost his/her power, the president, parliament, or dominant political party assumed the sovereign authority formerly exercised by the monarch.

As Stig Hadenius (1985:9-12) points out, in Sweden, for example, the instrument of government that remained in force until 1974 had been adopted in 1809. It stipulated that the country was a monarchy in which the King "alone" would govern the society. Members of the Swedish Riksdag (Parliament) nevertheless had the power to levy taxes and shared lawmaking power with the King. The Riksdag was divided into four estates--nobility, clergy, burghers, and peasants, reflecting the social and economic structure of a preindustrial society. This Riksdag, which had outlived its usefulness, was abolished in December 1865. The nobility no longer enjoyed the influence that had once clearly justified an estate of its own in the Riksdag, while many of the newer "aristocrats" of trade and industry lacked representation in any estate. The Riksdag of four estates was therefore replaced by a bicameral Riksdag that better reflected the changing power structure of Sweden.

4. Specialized Representation

This type of representation can be found in cases where representatives become both differentiated (specialized) and independent. As Andrain (1983:180) mentions, ancient government forms, like that in the Athenian city-state, made no clear distinction between representatives in the public and private spheres. The activities of these representatives were neither differentiated nor independent from other social groups such as leading families, the church, or economic associations. With the emergence of the nation-state, political activities came to be performed by more specialized representatives in legislatures, executives, administrations, and courts. These representatives also attempted to gain a functional autonomy from powerful primordial, religious, and economic groups.

5. Comprehensive Representation

This type of representation exists particularly in industrialized societies in which representatives exercise a wide scope of power; that is, they perform a comprehensive variety of activities: system maintenance, construction of an economic infrastructure, and provision of social services to individuals. According to Andrain (1983:180-181), when the modern nation-state first emerged during the fifteenth century, representatives concentrated on system maintenance--the preservation of the territorial integrity of the fragile nation-state. Representatives spent most of their time on public policies dealing with defense, foreign affairs, internal order, and the raising of revenues through levying taxes and printing a national currency.

At the beginning of the nineteenth century, Andrain further states, the construction of an economic infrastructure assumed greater importance as a distinctive activity of representatives. Policies designed by these representatives stimulated the construction of public works, such as roads, railways, and canals. Postal and telegraph services also spread. Subsidies were provided by representatives to promote agriculture, commerce, and industry.

During the twentieth century, and particularly after World War I, Andrain adds, the growing popularity of democratic values, the rising strength of socialist movements, the industrializing process, and the severe effects of the two world wars led representatives to design public policies that allocated social services to individuals. However, the advancement of industrialization, Andrain notes, made individuals become less self-sufficient. The growing specialization of labor, interdependence, and social personality stimulated popular demands for representatives to enact public policies that would meet individual needs. Therefore, since World War II, representatives in every modern democracy have spent an increasing share of public revenues on basic human needs programs: health, education, shelter, and food. All these services have helped to increase representatives' scope of power.

Conclusion

As the discussion in this chapter reveals, the suggestion that *action structure* is critical for understanding political behavior is hardly a matter of dispute. This structure, as we stated earlier, directs our attention to the occurrence of voting and representing and to the decision procedures through which such actions emerge. The acts of voting and representing in modern democracies occur in linear sequences: they are not randomly ordered; there is a pattern and a predictability to their occurrences. Furthermore, as we also stated earlier, acts of voting and representing are situated in a polity, such that what counts as a particular action is strongly constrained by what action precedes, what action is intended, what action is intended to follow, and what action actually does follow. As such, action structures are critical in fulfilling the ritual constraints of political behavior; that is, the interpersonal requirements of a democratic society.

It is not surprising therefore that all modern democracies emphasize voting as a major aspect of political participation. Voting is seen as an important source of power for citizens, and it does in fact allows them to remove incompetent, corrupt, or insensitive officials from office and to influence issues. However, voting has severe limitations as a means of exercising power. To begin with, the range of candidates that voters can choose from is limited because of the importance of political parties. Since the purposive behavior of all political parties is to win elections, normally, only candidates endorsed by the major parties have greater chances of winning political offices. As such, according to Maurice Duverger (1954), many groups are not effectively represented. The limited choice of political candidates is reinforced by the high cost of political

Action Structure

campaigns (as shown in chapter six). Only politicians who are wealthy enough to help finance their own campaigns or who are able to attract large financial contributions from supporters can mount effective campaigns. Such politicians are probably not representative of the public, and powerful contributors expect favors once the candidates whose campaigns they financed win political offices.

Representatives are approached to act as intermediaries to channel interests primarily because most citizens believe that a representative's voice is more effective than their own. The representatives are perceived by the public to be the overseers of the governmental establishment. The activities of the administrative agents are guided by the rules made by the representatives. Being most accessible, one's representative may be enlisted to channel interests to other elected representatives.

Chapter 4

Ideational Structure

Introduction

The limited scope of this chapter prevents us from extensively treating the subjects in this text; however, the intent of this chapter is: (1) to give a brief introduction into the nature and understanding of propositions and ideas, and (2) to relate the nature and context of these ideas and propositions to political behavior, namely, what can be seen as the result of the voters' and representatives' roles in negotiating their propositions for ideas, services, and goods. As stated in chapter one, three different relations between ideas contribute to the overall configuration of the ideational structure: (a) **Cohesive Relations** are established when a voter and a representative interpret an element in one proposition from a prior proposition because of the political relationship underlying them. (b) **Topic Relations** concern what a voter and a representative actually talk about on a given political transaction. (c) **Functional Relations** concern the roles ideas play in relation to one another and within the overall political context. For example, in a political district, some ideas for the quality of a particular representative or voter may serve as descriptive background for the quality of other representatives and voters.

Before proceeding, we must have a basic understanding of the nature of propositions and ideas. What can we know? What are the sources of knowledge? Where does genuine knowledge come from, or how do we know? What is the nature of knowledge? Is our knowledge valid? How do we distinguish truth from error? These are basic epistemological questions for any philosophical inquiry that is concerned with origins, appearance versus reality, and tests of truth, respectively. These questions are also necessary and sufficient conditions for the nature and context of ideas.

The foundation for all ideas is knowledge. What can we know about our ideas? What are the sources of our ideas? Where do genuine ideas come from, or how do we know that we even have an idea? What is the nature of ideas? Are our ideas valid? Is it possible to distinguish truth from error in an idea?

The Nature of Propositions

Propositions are either true or false and therefore differ from *questions, commands, and exclamations*. Grammarians classify the linguistic formulations of propositions, questions, commands, and exclamations as *declarative, interrogative, imperative, and exclamatory sentences,* respectively. It is important to distinguish between the declarative sentence and the proposition, because the declarative sentence is always part of a language, the language in which it is spoken or written, whereas propositions are not peculiar to any of the languages in which they may be expressed. According to Irvin Copi (1979:2-7) and R. Nelson (1989:282), another difference between declarative sentences and propositions is that the same sentence may be uttered in different contexts to assert different propositions.

Propositions are the basic components of *arguments*, and every argument has a structure, in the analysis of which the words *premise* or *conclusion* are usually employed. The *conclusion* of an argument is that proposition which is affirmed on the basis of other propositions of the argument. These *other propositions*, which are affirmed as providing grounds or reasons for accepting the conclusion, are the premises of the argument. Any proposition can either be a premise or a conclusion depending upon its context.

Furthermore, there must be some understanding as to whether the arguments containing these propositions are *deductive* or *inductive*. If the argument is deductive, then the related propositions provide conclusive grounds for its conclusion. In characterizing a deductive argument which has *true propositions*, it is proper to say that the argument is *sound* and *valid*, and it is *unsound* and *invalid* when at least one of the propositions is *false*. On the other hand, in characterizing an *inductive argument* which has true propositions, the related propositions claim only to provide some grounds for their conclusions. Inductive arguments are rarely referred to as valid or invalid, sound or unsound. These terms are usually assigned to deductive arguments. Inductive arguments are said to be *strong or weak, cogent or uncogent*. It is a common error to interchange these terms when classifying arguments and their propositions. Another common error is to relate an argument deductively when it is really an inductive argument.

Besides being either true or false, propositions also describe states of affairs. A state of affairs is *an event, experience, incident, occurrence, a phenomenon, or happening.* It is neither true nor false; it either occurs or it does not occur. The purpose of the proposition is to describe a state of affairs, and if it is true then it describes a state of affairs that did occur (past tense: *"I worked yesterday"*), that is occurring (present tense: *"I am presently working"*), or that will occur (future tense: *"I will work tomorrow"*). A proposition is false when it describes a state of affairs that did not occur, is not occurring, will not occur. States of affairs are never true, but propositions are either true or false.

Are there any absolute truths or falsities, or are truth and falsity always relative? Creating a similar example to that of Jacques P. Thiroux (1990:82-83), suppose we state the proposition, on November 7, 1994, *"We will vote tomorrow, November 8, 1994, in Prince George's County, Maryland's General Election."* In order to discover whether truth and falsity are relative or absolute, we need to ask what the status of this proposition is on the day we stated it (November 7, 1994). There are a number of possibilities to consider. At the time that we state the proposition, is it true until proven false or false until proven true? Is it true to me because we believe it and false to someone else because s/he does not believe it? Is it false or true because no one knows on November 7, 1994 whether we actually will vote on the following day? Or is it really neither true nor false because November 8, 1994 is not here yet?

Let us now suppose that it is November 8, 1994 and we cast our votes in Prince George's County, Maryland's General Election. Looking back to the proposition stated on November 7, 1994, was it not actually true when we stated it? On the other hand, if we do not vote on November 8, 1994 in Prince George's County, Maryland's General Election, then is it not the case that the proposition was false when we stated it on November 7, 1994? In other words, the proposition had to be either *true* or *false* when we stated it on November 7th; we just did not *know* it at the time which condition applied to it.

The point that we are trying to make, through Thiroux's example, is that truth does not stumble or lurk around because of time or because of what anyone believes or knows. Now, let us suppose as registered voters we believe it is true, but our representative (or candidate elect) does not. What difference does it make as to whether it is actually true or false? Also, on November 7, 1994 neither one of us knows it is either true or false; but, again, what difference does it make? None whatsoever--whether the proposition is true or false is based on whether or not the state of affairs actually occurs.

Truth and falsity, then, are indeed absolute. They do not switch around depending on expectation or belief, opportunity or time, feelings or opinions, or even knowledge. Propositions, according to Thiroux (1990:83), carefully and accurately stated, are not just true or false when they are stated, but are, in fact, true or false for all time.

Types of Propositions

It is important at this point to distinguish the difference between the types of propositions that can be used or misused. The most commonly used or misused propositions are the ***analytic, internal sense, external sense or empirical, and moral.*** These types of propositions are discussed separately.

Analytic Propositions

First, there are the ***analytic propositions.*** To formulate sound ideas and think clearly, we are obliged to accept the validity of certain laws

Ideational Structure

of thought. These include: **the Principle of Identity**, *"If p is true, then p is true"* (All A is A); **the Principle of Noncontradiction**, *"Not both p is true and p is false"* (Not both A and not A); and **the Principle of Excluded Middle**, *"p is either true or false"* (Either A or not A). To deny the truth of this type of proposition would be to contradict oneself; given the meanings and definitions of the words of these propositions, that is, what *p* represents, they are absolute truths, and we know that they are. For example, **the Principle of Identity**, *"If it is the case that Bill Clinton is President, then it is true that Bill Clinton is President;"* **the Principle of Noncontradiction**, *"Not both Bill Clinton is the President and it is not the case that Bill Clinton is the President;* **the Principle of Excluded Middle**, *"Either Bill Clinton is the President or it is not the case that Bill Clinton is the President."* Given the definition and understanding of the terms in each of the propositions for the Principle of Noncontradiction and Excluded Middle, it is not logically possible that a term could be affirmed in one case and then the same term denied in the other. Also, assuming that *p* stands for something other than the examples used, it is a basic and ultimate truth or principle of logic that whatever else may or may not be said truly about anything, a thing must by its very definition be what it is (i.e. equivalent to itself). Therefore, any analytic proposition is a truth that is known to be absolute.

There are four basic standard forms to analytic proposition. They are: the A-form, *Universal Affirmative*; the E-form, *Universal Negative*; the I-form, *Particular Affirmative*; and the O-form, *Particular Negative*. The *quality* of a proposition is said to be *affirmative* if it asserts class members and is said to be *negative* if it denies class members. The **quantity** of a proposition is said to be **universal** if it makes a claim that each and every member of the S class is a member of the P class (as do *"All S is P,"* and *"No S is P"*), and **particular** if it makes a claim that some or at least one of the class of S is a member of the class P (as do *"Some S is P,"* and *"Some S is not P"*). Every good proposition contains two categories or classes known as *the subject* and *the predicate* conjoined by some conjugation of the verb *"to be,"* called the **copula**. Thus, the A-form proposition is represented as *"All S is P,"* the E-form proposition is represented as *"No S is P,"* the I-form proposition is represented as *"Some S is P,"* and the O-form proposition is represented as *"Some S* *is not P."* In each case, it is understood that *S* and *P* stands for something; that is, *S* and *P* represent either a class, group, set, category, or genre.

The A-form proposition, the ***Universal Affirmative***, purports that *"All S is P,"* that is to say that each and every member of *S* is a member of *P*. For example, *"All United States Presidents are men,"* is to say that each and every President of the United States is a man, but it is not saying that each and every man in the United States is a President. This process is called *distribution*, and we can see that only the *subject* is distributed in the A-form. Similarly, the E-form proposition, ***the Universal Negative***, purports that *"No S is P,"* that is to say that no members of *S* is a member of *P*. For example, *"No United States Presidents are women,"* is to say also that, *"No women are United States Presidents;"* in other words the *subject* and the *predicate* of the E-form are distributed (since both propositions are equivalent). The I-form proposition, ***the Particular Affirmative***, may be stated thus, *"Some S are P,"* which actually purports that there is at least one member of *S* that is a *P*. For example, *"Some United States Presidents are Republicans,"* says that at least one United States President is also a Republican, but this propositional form has ***no distribution*** in either the *subject or the predicate*. This can be seen in the fact that although the proposition *"Some Republicans are United States Presidents,"* may be true, it is not an equivalent relation, because the latter is concern with the one member of the republican party that is also President while the former is concerned with the one individual of the class of Presidents that is also a Republican. Finally, there is the O-form proposition, ***Particular Negative***, which purports that *"Some S is not P."* For example, *"Some United States Presidents are not Republicans,"* which actually states that there is at least one United States President that is not a Republican (Copi 1979:83).

These four propositions may be represented in pictorial form called *Venn Diagrams*. The **A-form proposition** may be represented by

Ideational Structure

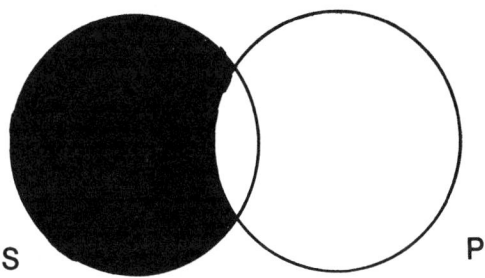

The **E-form proposition** may be represented by

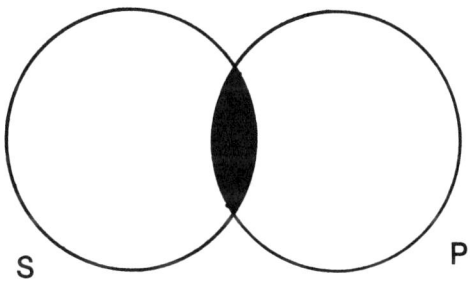

The **I-form proposition** may be represented by

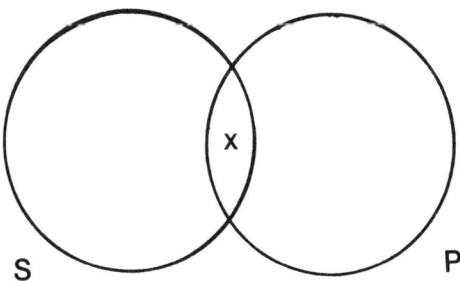

The **O-form proposition** may be represented by

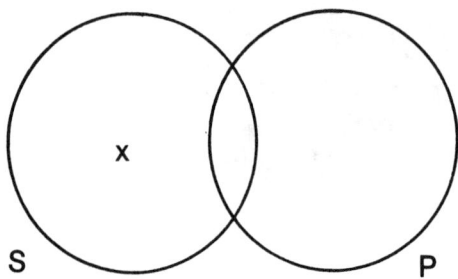

The Basics of Quantification Theory

Determining the truth or falsity and consequently the validity of the standard form proposition can be done in several ways, but it is sufficient to discuss at this point a few of the most important ones: ***Quantification Theory and the Square of Opposition and their Relation to Venn Diagrams*** and ***the Rules of Inference.***

Quantification theory allows one to speak of the validity of any compound or non-compound statements and symbolize their structures. For example,

All democrats are mortal.
Bill Clinton is democrat.
Therefore, Bill Clinton is mortal.

This syllogism (i.e. a three-categorical proposition) shows the use of compound and non-compound propositions, both in standard form proposition and singular proposition. We recall that standard form propositions, such as the A-form, have a ***subject term*** and a ***predicate term***. In the first premise, the A-form, the subject term is humans and the predicate term is mortal. But, the second and third premises are not in one of the standard forms (A, E, I, or O). The second and third premises are known as singular propositions, and any (Affirmative) singular proposition states that the individual referred to by its subject term is said to have the attribute designated by its predicate term. It is customary to speak of the attributes of individual things, such as

Ideational Structure 59

cities, animals, chemicals, tables, chairs, or places, as well as persons as things. Attributes may either be adjectives, verbs, or even nouns.

When we symbolize singular propositions, we use the letters *'a'* through *'w'* to denote the individuals, ordinarily using the first letter of an individual's name to denote the individual. These symbols are called '**individual constants**.' Attributes are designated by capital letters. Therefore, using our preceding argument, we denote Bill Clinton by a small letter *'s'* and symbolize the attributes human and mortal by the capital letters *'H'* and *'M.'* It is customary when expressing a singular proposition to write the symbol for its predicate term to the left of the symbol for its subject term. Thus, we symbolize *'Bill Clinton is democrat'* as *'Hs'* and *'Bill Clinton is mortal'* as *'Ms.'*

When considering the class of all singular propositions that have the same structure as our example above, we use the expression *'Hx'* to symbolize the pattern common to all such singular propositions. The lower case letter *'x'* is called an '**individual variable.**' It is important to remember that according to our established symbolic formulation, singular propositions of the form *'Ha'*, *'Hb'*, *'Hc'*,..., *'Hw'* are either true or false; but *'Hx'* is neither true nor false, since it is not a proposition. These types of expression are called '**propositional functions.**' These are expressions that contain individual variables and become propositions when their individual variables are replaced by individual constants. The process of obtaining a proposition from a propositional function by substituting a constant for a variable is called '**instantiation.**' Any singular proposition can be regarded as 'substitution instance' of the propositional function from which it results by the substitution of an individual constant for the individual variable in the propositional function. The negative singular propositions *'Bush is not honest'* and *'Reagan is not honest,'* symbolized *'~Hb'* and *'~Hr,'* result by instantiation from the propositional function *'Hx,'* of which they are substitution instances.

Now we have the tools to symbolize how any general proposition, such as *'Everyone is democratic'* and *'Someone is democratic,'* differs from singular propositions in that they do not contain the names of individuals. They can, however, be regarded as resulting from propositional functions, not by instantiation, but by *'generalization'* or *'quantification.'* The first example, *'Everyone is democratic,'* can be alternatively expressed as

Given any individual person whomever, s/he is democratic.

Here, the pronoun *'s/he'* refers back to the word *'everyone.'* We can use the individual variable *'x'* in place of the pronoun *'s/he'* and its antecedent to paraphrase the first general proposition as

Given any x, x is democratic.

Now we can use the notation already introduced to rewrite it as

Given any x, Dx.

The phrase *'Given any x'* is called a **'universal quantifier'** and is symbolized by *'(x).'* Combining this new symbol with already established notations, we can completely symbolize our general proposition as follows:

(x)Dx

We can, similarly, paraphrase the second general proposition, *'Someone is democratic,'* successively as

There is at least one person that is democratic.
There is at least one person such that s/he is democratic.
There is at least one x such that x is democratic.

This can also be stated as

There is at least one x such that Dx.

The phrase *'There is at least one x such that'* is called an **'existential quantifier'** and is symbolized as *'($\exists$x).'* Using our new symbol, we can completely symbolize our second general proposition as

($\exists$x)Dx

Therefore, a general proposition is formed from a propositional function by placing either a universal or an existential quantifier

Ideational Structure

before it. Thus, the universal quantification of a propositional function is true, if and only if all its substitution instances are true. Likewise, the existential quantification of a propositional function is true, if and only if has at least one true substitution instance. If we agree that there is at least one individual, then every propositional function has at least one substitution instance (true or false). Also, if the universal quantification of propositional function is true, then its existential quantification must be true as well. The general connections between universal and existential quantification can be described in the following square array, called the **Quantification Theory Array:**

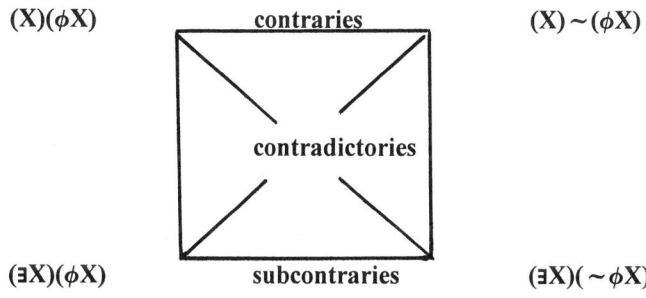

Assuming the existence of at least one individual, the normal convention is to say that the two top propositions are **contraries** (i.e. they can and might both be false, but cannot both be true). The two bottom propositions are **subcontraries** (i.e. they can and might both true, but cannot both be false). The propositions that are at opposite ends of the diagonals are called **contradictories**, of which one must be true and the other must be false. Finally, on each side, the truth of the lower proposition is implied by the truth of the proposition directly above it. This relation is called **alternation**. The basis for this Quantification Theory Array is the Square of Opposition supposedly developed by Aristotle.

Now, it is possible to rephrase the traditional four types of subject-predicate propositions mentioned earlier (i.e. *A-form, E-form, I-form, and E-form*). For instance,

All voters are democrats.
No voters are democrats.
Some voters are democrats.
Some voters are not democrats.

Thus, the **A**-form proposition may be paraphrased as

> Given any individual thing whatever, if it is a voter, then it is democrat.
> Given any x, if x is a voter, then x is democrat.
> Given any x, x is a voter ⊃x is democrat.

Finally, it can be symbolized as

$$(x)(Vx \supset Dx)$$

The **E** proposition, 'No voters are democrats,' may similarly be paraphrased successively as

> Given any individual thing whatever, if it is a voter, then it is not democrat.
> Given any x, if x is a voter, then x is not democrat.
> Given any x, x is a voter ⊃x is not democrat.

It can be symbolized as

$$(x)(Vx \supset {\sim}Dx)$$

Similarly, the **I** proposition, *'Some voters are democrats,'* may be paraphrased as

> There is at least one thing that is a voter and democrat.
> There is at least one thing such that it is human and it is democrat.
> There is at least one x such that x is a voter and x is democrat.
> There is at least one x such that x is a voter · x is democrat.

It can completely be symbolized as

$$(\exists x)(Vx \cdot Dx)$$

Ideational Structure

Finally, the **O** proposition, *'Some voters are not democrats,'* becomes

> There is at least one thing that is a voter, but not democrat.
> There is at least one such thing that it is a voter and it is not democrat.
> There is at least one x such that x is a voter and · x is not democrat.

It can then be symbolized as the existential quantification of a complex function as follows:

$$(\exists x)(Vx \cdot \sim Dx)$$

The Greek letters Φ and Ψ are used to symbolize any attribute, and the four standard subject-predicate propositions of traditional logic may be represented in a **Square Array** as follows:

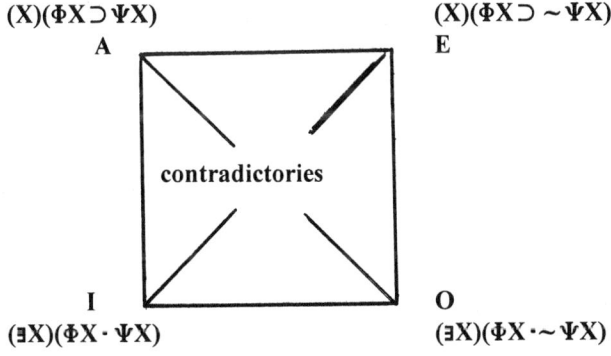

This **Square Array** must not be confused with the **Square of Opposition**, although there are some similarities. In the array above, the **A** and the **O** are contradictories, and the **E** and the **I** are contradictories also. That is as far as it goes for the relationships discussed in terms of quantification versus traditional standard form propositions discussed earlier.

Where 'Φ*x*' is a proposition function that has no true substitution instances, then regardless of what attribute is symbolized by Ψ the propositional functions Φx then Ψx' and Φx then ~Ψx' have only true substitution instances. This is so because all their substitution instances are conditional statements with false antecedents. In such cases both the **A** and **E** propositions that are the universal quantifications of these complex propositional functions are true, so **A** and **E** propositions are not contraries (in the traditional sense meaning that both cannot be true). Again, where $\Phi x'$ is a propositional function that has no true substitution instances, then regardless of what $\Psi x'$ might be, the propositional functions Φx and $\Psi x'$ and Φx and $\sim\Psi x'$ have only false substitution instances, for their substitution instances are conjunctions whose first conjuncts are false. In such cases, the **I** and the **O** propositions that are the existential quantifications of these complex propositional functions are false. Thus, the **I** and the **O** propositions are not subcontraries (in the traditional sense, meaning that both cannot be false). In all such cases, then, since the **A** and **E** propositions are true and the **I** and the **O** propositions are false, the truth of the universal does not imply the truth of the corresponding particular; no implication relation holds between them.

If we make the assumption that there is at least one individual, then $'(x)(\Phi x \supset \Psi x)'$ does not imply $'(\exists x \ni)(\Phi x \supset \Psi x)'$. The latter, however, is not an **I** proposition. An **I** proposition of the form 'Some Φ's and Ψ's' is symbolized as $'(\exists x \ni)(\Phi x \cdot \Psi x),'$ which asserts that there is at least one thing having both the attribute Φ and the attribute Ψ. But the proposition $'(\exists x \ni)(\Phi x \supset \Phi s)'$ asserts only that there is at least one object that either has the attribute Ψ or does not have the attribute Φ, which is a very different and much 'weaker' assertion.

The Rules of Inference for Propositions

With most systems of reasoning that involve ideas and propositions, there are rules that govern and guide the process. We will discuss four of the most common rules that seem to be frequented in the ideational structure. The first of these is **Modus Ponens (MP)**, which is

$$p \supset q$$
$$p$$
$$\overline{}$$
$$q$$

Ideational Structure

An argument having this form is a valid argument form (P. J. Hurley 1993:337). Example:

If Martin Luther King is assassinated, then Martin Luther King is dead. Martin Luther King is assassinated. Therefore, Martin Luther King is dead. This can be symbolized as follows:

$$M \supset D$$
$$M$$
$$\overline{D}$$

The MP is of the form where the first proposition is conditional, the second proposition asserts the antecedent (M) of the first conditional proposition, and a conclusion that asserts the consequent (D).

An invalid form of the MP is the **Fallacy of Affirming the Consequent (AC)**, and it is stated as

If Bill Clinton is a racist, then Bill Clinton is president.
Bill Clinton is president. Therefore, Bill Clinton is a racist.

It can be symbolized as

$$B \supset P$$
$$P$$
$$\overline{B}$$

Any argument that has the form of affirming the consequent (AC) is an invalid argument (Hurley 1993:338). We assert that an argument has an *invalid* form if it can be produced by uniformly substituting statements in place of the variables in an invalid form *and* it cannot be produced by uniformly substituting statements in place of the variables in any valid form.

A second valid argument form is **Modus Tollens (MT)**. MT consists of one conditional proposition or premise, a second proposition or premise that denies the consequent of the conditional proposition or premise. The conclusion of the MT denies the antecedent as follows:

$$B \supset S$$
$$\sim S$$
$$\overline{\sim B}$$

If Baghdad cares about Kuwait, then it has stopped invading Kuwait. Baghdad has not stopped invading Kuwait. Therefore, Baghdad does not care about Kuwait.

Similarly, there is an invalid form associated with MT, the **Fallacy of Denying the Antecedent (DA)**. Denying the antecedent consists of a conditional premise, a second premise that denies the antecedent of the conditional, and a conclusion that denies the consequent as follows (Hurley 1993:339):

$$p \supset q$$
$$\sim p$$
$$\overline{\sim q}$$

Any argument that has the form of denying the antecedent is an invalid argument (Hurley 1993:339). For example,

If the NAACP provides full disclosure of its finances to the public, then the NAACP is an honest organization. The NAACP does not provide full disclosure of its finances to the public. Therefore, the NAACP is not an honest organization.

This can be represented as follows:

$$N \supset H$$
$$\sim N$$
$$\overline{\sim H}$$

Again, this argument has true propositions (premises) and a false conclusion, so it is clearly invalid (Hurley 1993:339).

A third valid form of the propositional argument is the **Hypothetical Syllogism**. It is stated as follows:

If I represent myself in court, then I have a fool for a lawyer. But if I have a fool for a lawyer, then I have a fool for a client. So if I represent myself in court, then I have a fool for a client.

This can be symbolized as

$$R \supset L$$
$$L \supset C$$
$$\overline{R \supset C}$$

What this set of propositions assert is that if R is a sufficient condition for L, and L is a sufficient condition for C, then R is a sufficient condition for C. Or, again, if C is a necessary condition for L (second premise [proposition]), and L is a necessary condition for R (first premise [proposition]), then C is a necessary condition for R.

The fourth valid form is the **Disjunctive Syllogism** (W. H. Halberstadt 1974:49-50). A disjunctive proposition is of the form '$P \vee Q$.' Actually, the English word "or" is ambiguous; sometimes it means "and/or," and sometimes it means "either...or...but not both." This is important in ideational structure as we will discuss later, in that, in the first sense, in which at least one of the disjuncts (these being the statements on each side of the "or") is true, and in which the possibility that both may be true is not excluded, we say that the "or" is "an inclusive disjunctive." However, in the second case, only one of the disjuncts is true, the "or" is referred to as "an exclusive disjunction" (Halberstadt 1974:49-50).

If someone says, hypothetically, *"Your representative can vote for the peace referendum at the House or the Senate,"* that person is using an inclusive disjunction and probably does not mean to imply that you can not vote for the referendum at the House and the Senate. You probably will not vote at both places, but you very well could. All that the inclusive disjunctive statement implies is that one or the other representatives may vote or perhaps both representatives in the House and Senate may vote.

On the other hand, if someone says that the representative is either a Democrat or Republican, that person is using an exclusive disjunction, since, technically speaking, no representative can be listed as both a Democrat and a Republican. If, for example, we are given an inclusive disjunct of the form '$P \vee Q$,' and we are further told that one disjunct is not the case, then we may conclude that one disjunct is the case. This principle is symbolized as

$$P \vee Q$$
$$\sim P$$
$$\overline{Q}$$

Another example of this form yields us,

> Either I will vote for representative **Q** or I will vote for representative **S**. I will not vote for representative **Q**. Therefore, I will vote for representative **S**.

This statement may be symbolized as

$$Q \vee S$$
$$\sim Q$$
$$\overline{S}$$

Internal Sense Propositions

The *internal sense propositions* are propositions that we assert, as human beings, about our internal homeostases (feelings, moods, emotions, temperament, passions, etc.,); for example, *"My feet ache," "I feel uncomfortable," "I am in a bad mood," "I love music."* If these propositions are honestly spoken, then they are always true because we alone truly know our own internal states. You might say *"I feel depressed,"* and a doctor, nurse, therapist, and minister might tell you that there is no reason for you feeling the way that you do. However, that does not negate the fact that you feel miserable. Only you know whether you do or not. This type of propositions then state truths that we know are absolute. These propositions can be known to be true in what John Hospers (1967:151) calls the *'strong sense of knowing,'* which fulfills the following requirements:

1. I must believe the proposition is true.

Ideational Structure

2. The proposition must actually be true.

3. I must have absolutely conclusive evidence that it is true (D. D. Runes 1955:84).

The interpretation of these requirements and their importance to ideational structure will be dealt with latter in this chapter. However, it is sufficient to present them now.

Empirical or External Sense Propositions

There is an *empirical or external sense* type of proposition. This type of proposition is different from the first two (i.e. analytic and internal sense) in that it describes a state of affairs that occurs in the external world. We can verify the validity of this information directly by way of our senses (seeing, tasting, smelling, hearing, touching), and indirectly by way of reasoning. *"This candidate for mayor is the best dressed in the race," "He is an African-American," "This President does not have a foreign policy," "This food is spoiled"* are examples of empirical propositions. Whether empirical propositions can be proven to be absolutely true has been the debate of philosophers down through the centuries. Some empirical propositions can be known to be absolutely true or false. For example, if the light is good, if your eyes are normal, if you understand what the words you are using mean, and if you have carefully examined the individual in front of you and have found this person to be an African-American, then the statement, *"He is an African-American,"* would seem to be an absolutely true proposition that you know to be true. So, for the purpose of this chapter, at least, we will assume that some empirical propositions can be known to be true and, therefore, that there are some empirical propositions that are absolutely true.

Moral Propositions

Moral propositions are those statements that have ethical import. A moral proposition differs from the other three in that it contains value judgments about the morality of human actions or character. This type of proposition often contains words such as *good, bad, evil, right, wrong, should, ought, just, and unjust*, etc. Some examples of this type of proposition are *"The death penalty is an unjust and unusual punishment;" " Human beings should never kill other human beings except in self defense;" "Martin Luther King, Jr., John F. Kennedy, and Mohandas Gandhi were good men;" "Patient-assisted suicide is the same as murder."* The important issue for this type of proposition is its ethical import, because this distinction separates it from all other propositions. Are moral propositions ever absolutely true? Furthermore, can any human being know whether they are or are not? According to Thiroux, moral propositions have only *'emotive or non-cognitive meanings'* (Runes 1955:85); they only express attitudes or feelings. Moral propositions are either voicing their approval or disapproval of an entity, trying to evoke some feeling or attitude in others. John Hospers, on the other hand, sees moral propositions as having more than just an emotive meaning (Hospers 1967:114-121). He sees moral propositions as having three aspects:

1. The purpose or the intention of the person or persons who utter them.

2. The effect the propositions have on their hearers.

3. The actual meaning of the propositions (Hospers 1983:526-593).

(Again, this is very important to ideational structure; however, it is sufficient to present this information at this point and provide the interpretation later). Nevertheless, the general problem with moral propositions is the emotive factor that is weaved within some of its content. One can not help but think that most statements that include value judgments will, by their nature, carry with them some deeply-held beliefs prompting in some cases an emotive response in defense of these beliefs.

Another factor associated with moral propositions is a tendency to be prescriptive. If moral propositions are not evoking an emotive response, they are prescribing or telling the hearer what s/he should in fact be doing. For example, *"Every human being should follow the*

Golden Rule or The Ten Commandments," "People who commit heinous crimes should receive the death penalty," "A woman ought to have an abortion for any reason she thinks necessary," "Young people who commit serious crimes should be charged as adults." These statements certainly assert something about reality and also include a value judgment as part of that assertion. But, can they ever be considered as true or false? This type of moral proposition becomes a dominant theme of candidates and representatives during an election period to foster an emotive response from potential voters.

Selecting Propositions

It is quite possible that the voter and or the representative might be expected to compose a proposition for either an argument or a policy statement. Although there is some disagreement of opinion, according to John C. Reinard (1991:59-70), most scholars would agree that the following guidelines for selecting propositions are desirable:

1. **The proposition should be significant enough to warrant argument, discussion, and/or debate**. Such a proposition should be vital, important, and interesting. The topic should be important enough that serious thought on it is possible and its relevance to society's important needs is visible.

2. **The proposition should be suitable for the advocates and their audience**. Although topics such as the growth of democracy in Haiti, the governmental policies of Nelson Mandela, the increase of teen pregnancies in America, and violent crimes in the United States are important and should be debated, the issue remains that the topic should be one that is of importance to the listener.

3. **The proposition should be controversial**. People generally do not debate nor argue topics such as *"Resolved: that water freezes at 32 degrees Fahrenheit or zero degrees Centigrade."* Such matters are capable of direct demonstration. Instead, one should choose topics where an honest difference of opinion leaves room for controversy.

4. **The proposition should deal with one idea**. More than one idea makes the proposition too awkward to permit sensible discussion. Topics should deal with one idea. Propositions of the form '$A \cdot B$,' '$A \vee B$,' and '$A \vee (B \cdot C)$,' contain more than one proposition, that is, 'A,' 'B,' 'C,' and should be treated separately.

5. **The proposition should be of current interest**. Whenever possible, it is wise for the voter and the representative to select propositions that reflect the times because people will want to discuss the topic before the time has passed.

Of course, one should understand that these guidelines are not the only ones that might be used. In a more formal setting, such as townhall meetings, debates, and platform discussions, the voter and representative might establish guidelines very similar to the one above, but with some exceptions as follows:

1. The proposition should involve and interest both voter and representative.

2. The proposition should be nationally controversial.

3. The proposition should stimulate the opportunity for opposing views from both voter and representative. Equal time should be given for these views.

4. The proposition should stimulate research to produce ample evidence for both points of view.

5. The proposition should be in the language of subject-matter experts.

The Language of Propositions

The standards of writing and critical thinking should be kept in mind when preparing to phrase a proposition. Critical thinking is the careful and deliberate effort to make a decision about a proposition based on thoughtful evaluation of available information. It involves carefully isolating and weighing the issues of a proposition and then making some decision. When one is acting critically, one adopts a scientific attitude and brings the force of available information to bear on the decision. However, there are some special considerations and guidelines that should be considered to avoid confusion, ambiguity, and misrepresentation of the facts. According to Reinard (1991:63-64), the following guidelines are acceptable:

1. **Propositions should be in declarative sentences.** To have clear direction for any proposition, it should be a declarative sentence rather than asking a question.

2. **Propositions should be free of "loaded" language.** We once received a questionnaire from our representative to Congress that was so filled with loaded language that a fair statement for disagreement was impossible. One question asked if we thought the "President should support expanded military funding in the best interests of the United States' national defense." Such a proposition was so loaded with inflammatory language that it invited its own answer. Such loaded language makes propositions of little use since they cloud the discussion with irrelevancies.

3. **Propositions should be clearly phrased.** Rather than vague descriptions, such as *"Resolved: that the United States should do something about terrorism,"* one might wish to state clearly what that 'something' is.

4. **Propositions of policy should propose change in beliefs or policies.** The voter or representative should not propose or ask to adopt a program that arouses deeply-held beliefs. Rather, the voter or representative should argue propositions that ask to consider changes to different policies.

5. **Propositions of policy should be phrased to state the types of changes advocated.** The direction and nature of the change should be stated in useful propositions. Especially between voter and representative during informal arguments, when the proposition is

unclear, the arguers may waste time discussing irrelevant points in the proposition.[9]

When the propositions are carefully selected and phrased, it is likely that productive debate might occur. It might be wise to consider the impact that a proposition may have on cohesive relations, topic relations, and functional relations. Although guidelines and strategies for propositions are available, such as the ones stated above, in negotiating the proposition, the voters and representatives can develop conflicts over behaviors and strongly disagree with one another. Reinard suggests a model that was developed by Sara E. Newell and Randall Strutman who studied this type of interpersonal phenomena over a three-year period. They found that these social confrontations could be mapped out with great accuracy. Finding a way to settle the disagreement is a critical part of analyzing the proposition by both voter and representative. This model is shown in the Figure 2 (Reinard 1991:64-65).

The question involves objectionable behavior of the other party, not just a disagreement over ideas. To analyze an episode, one must answer six potential questions. If the answer is *"yes,"* the controversy ends. If the answer is *"no,"* then the arguers (i.e. the voters and/or the representatives) must thrash out the issue before proceeding. Of course, voters and/or representatives may jump from one issue to another, but this model describes what usually occurs in these social confrontation episodes (i.e. the social and political conflicts over behaviors of arguers [e.g., voters and representatives]).

---

[9]The word *'should'* in propositions means *'ought to but not necessarily will.'* This meaning indicates that proponents are not required to prove that a proposition will be accepted by other voters or representatives. The merits or demerits of a proposition may be judged without the need to show the likelihood of adoption of the proposition. One must examine propositions to determine if, in context, the word *'should'* means *'ought to'* or a simple value expression.

Figure 2:
Confrontation Over Behaviors:
Analysis of Social Confrontation Episodes

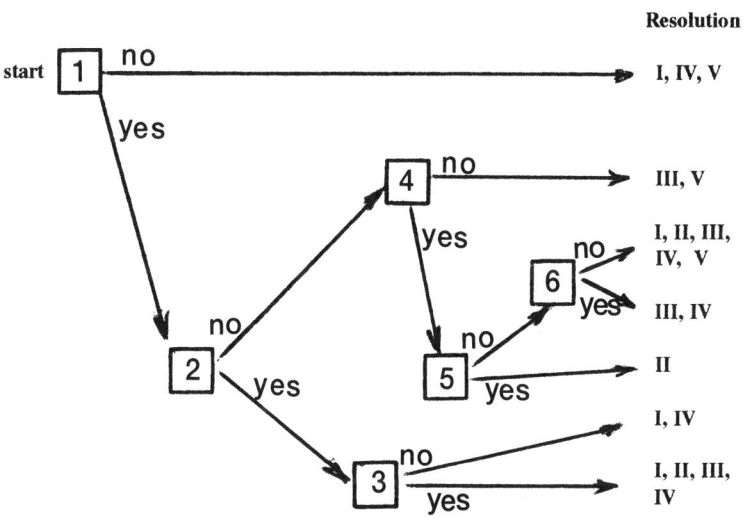

1. Is the implied rule mutually accepted as legitimate?
2. Is this a special situation?
3. If invoked, is the superceding rule mutually accepted as legitimate?
4. Did the accused (i.e., voter or representative) actually perform the behavior in question?
5. Does the behavior constitute a violation of the rule?
6. Does the accused (i.e., voter or representative) accept responsibility for the behavior?

Methods of Resolution:
I. Legislation   II. Remediation   III. Reaffirmation
IV. Remedy   V. No Resolution

In conjunction with Newell and Stutman's research, Reinard[10] concludes that there are five ways to settle disputes over behavior. The first of these is the remedy, in which one arguer agrees to take actions to make up for the problem. These steps may include: stopping the offending behavior, showing remorse or sadness over causing problems, offering to redress or repair damages, or accepting punishment. The second way is **legislation,** in which both parties agree to come up with a new rule to be followed by both parties in the future. The third family of settlements involves **remediation**, in which an existing rule is not rejected but is further defined or amended to prevent future misunderstandings. Fourth, **reaffirmation** may occur, in which each participation agrees that the existing rule is acceptable and promises to follow it in the future. Finally, of course, it is possible that **no resolution** is possible. The problem may be *put on hold* or just ignored.

Propositions: The Desirability-Probability Interaction

Propositions become increasingly persuasive as they are used because the language suggests desirability, which in turn influence our belief in their probable truth (Reinard 1991:66-67). If we hear a proposition that states that *"the federal government should guarantee health care assistance for every American,"* it may sound very desirable to many of us.

General research on desirability and probability has supported such a position. Research has shown a positive relationship between a person's rating the proposition as desirable and a person's rating the *"probability of belief found in it"* (Reinard 1991:66). Similarly, it has been found that the perceived truth of logical argument is affected by how desirable the argument's claim sounds to either the voter or the representative. If the language used in phrasing a proposition is compelling to the ear, the amount of argument needed to prove the proposition may not be great. If the concepts strike a consistent chord

---

[10]John C. Reinard does not explain why he disagrees with the solution order of Methods of Resolution established by Sara E. Newell and Randall Stutman. However, Reinard's method is as logical in the way that it is presented. It should and can be used as an alternative approach.

with the audience's basic values, the very phrasing of the proposition actually may contribute to its persuasiveness.

Some representatives and candidates for public office, primarily in the quest for either re-election or election, tend to think about issues and propositions monolithically. The tendency is to see issues in life as all good or all bad. Words may carry positive or negative evaluations and propositions that contain positive words are most easily learned.

Propositions employing negative phrases seem difficult for most folks to comprehend. According to Reinard (1991:67)[11], it is known that negative propositions are harder than affirmative ones to grasp, both in terms of the time taken to understand them and the errors involved in so doing.

Given that propositions can be misinterpreted due to language, context, and behavior, is there a process that can assist one in analyzing the propositions in question? According to Reinard (1991:89-92), there are at least two approaches to discovering the issues for argument.

The Stock Issues Approach. Stock issues consist of a set of questions that have stood the test of time. In brief, the system poses five types of questions:

1. **Questions of need or advantage** are raised. The question often asked, *"Is there a warrant for change?"* is sometimes recognized as the issue of significance.

2. **Questions of inherence** are also addressed. To establish a warrant to reject the present system, the problem also must be shown to be inherent to the present system. An inherent situation is one that has been caused by the essential nature of the present system.

---

[11] John Reinard quotes Jerry Boucher and Charles Osgood who label this tendency to only see good as the Pollyanna Hypothesis, named after the children's story character who preferred to see good rather than bad things in life.

3. **Questions of solvency** are probed by asking the following: Is there a plan that can solve the problem area identified in the warrant change? Those who advance a proposition must demonstrate that a plan could affect the present situation in a practicable and effective manner.

4. **Questions of disadvantages** involve asking whether the advantages of the planned change outweigh the accompanying disadvantages. A disadvantage is a harm created by the plan suggested by a policy proposition. If the disadvantages are worst than the advantages, then there is reason to reject the proposition. But if the disadvantages do not out weigh the advantages, then there remains some justification for accepting changes.

5. **Questions of feasibility** may be important matters for arguments. These questions do not refer to the desirability or effectiveness of a plan, merely to its possibility for existence. These questions involve whether a plan is technologically possible.

Proponents of a proposition are responsible for showing that there is just cause for a change and that there is a plan of action that would affect the deficiencies identified. Opponents, on the other hand, typically introduce arguments on the last two types of questions above.

The Systems Approach. According to Reinard (1991:92-93), this approach is based on the extensive work of Ludwig von Bertalanffy. When a controversy is not sufficiently focused to permit the statement of a proposition for a specific course of action, the system approach might be invited. When a group of community leaders asks whether action should be taken to curb the national drug epidemic, the question may not be perceived as a proposition such as "Resolved: that all government workers should be subject to mandatory drug testing." Instead, the question may be "Which program for reducing the use of drugs has the greatest merit?" The following process may isolate some issues:

1. **Isolating the system** is the first step in system analysis. A system is defined as an entity which functions as an entity because of the interdependence of its elements. When members of Congress

make an effort to decide if national health care should be implemented, they may try to define the health care system in terms of a system by which people can pay for health care directly or through insurance programs.

2. **System components** are important to the overall operation and must be identified within the system in order to divide the system into some recognizable parts. If Congress considered adopting national health care insurance, it would be wise for its members to recognize the health care system's components: administrative providers, physicians, support staff, hospitals, patients, and medical specialists.

3. **System interrelationships** are isolated. Perhaps more than anything else, systems are distinctive because of the relationships among components. The administrative providers (health insurance companies and hospital components) have interacted to increase medical costs, since many insurance programs pay benefits only when expensive hospital care is involved.

4. **System goals** are key to the activities of the systems. Systems are goal directed and analysts must determine those system purposes. The process of determining system goals has two aspects: (a) the discovery of the stated or implied goals of the existing system and (b) the determination of optimum system goals. The contrast between what the goals of the system should be and what the goals actually are; this, in turn, may invite argument about the degree to which the gap between the two is significant.

5. **Effect assessments** are part of the systems approach. Since a system viewpoint holds that a change in one part of a system carries with it a change for the entire system, the nature of these effects must be assessed to determine (a) if the changes could remove deficiencies, and (b) if they would entail more costs than benefits.

6. **System management** is the part of the system that controls the activity within it. The management of a system shapes it and

influences how things really will work in practice.

When looking at both the stock issues and the systems approaches, one might notice some striking similarities. The systems issues perspective can best be considered a way of complementing the stock issues approach, rather than a fundamental rejection of it.

The Nature of Idea

The etymology of the word **idea** is from three Greek words *idea*, which means *"concept," "class," "kind," "mode," "sort," "species," "form," "nature,"* from *eidos*, which means *"visual appearance," "form,"* and *idein*, which means *"to see," "to grasp conceptually"* (P. A. Angeles 1981:119). Thus, any object or item, whether visual or ontological, that is a content of consciousness is called an *idea*. This consciousness precipitates an awareness of *form* and *image*, both linguistically and conceptually, in the mind. A *mental image or picture* of an item or object is formed and words are structured to formulate a statement about the object or item that is being conceived ontologically. The picture or mental image that is constructed in the mind may very well be a real entity or purely metaphysical in nature. However, for the sake of the content in this chapter, the images and pictures will be confined to the real.

When an idea is presented either as a real likeness, representation, or essence of an item embodied in an object, the thing or object takes on the physical attributes of the idea. This process is sometimes a tedious one, but necessary, to construct a segment of imagination into reality and move from the intangible to the tangible. In many cases, this idea began either as a mental image or a picture of something. For an idea to be accepted, it must either move or flow from mind to matter, from the ontological to the visual, and from thought to language. It is true that an idea may be fantasized, fictionalized, and supposed, but the idea most accepted is the one that moves from the mind to matter (i.e. concrete or visual evidence).

In ideational structure, however, ideas are sometimes presented as beliefs, opinions, suppositions, or dogma (Angeles 1981:119). From what sources do ideas originate? Are ideas generated externally or internally? According to W. G. Hegel, an idea is the unity of subject and object (W. T. Stace 1944:77). He arrives at this conclusion in typical dialectical method. First he states the **thesis**, *'The nature of reality of the world is essentially subject'*; then he states the **antithesis**, *'Reality is now defined as the opposite of subject, namely object'*; and the **synthesis**, *'The defining of reality as being, the unity of subject and object.'* Thus, the idea is further defined as the unity of subjectivity (knowing) and objectivity (being) (Stace 1955:279-280).

According to H. H. Titus (1970:50-51), ideas are the projection of our thoughts onto the outer world. This description denotes what is known as the *egocentric* predicament, that is, no matter what we do or how hard we try, we can never go beyond our own experience. All our knowledge of objects are of the subject-object variety. When we think of an object, we think of it in some sensorially perceived qualities. The object is sweet, sour, large, or smooth.

Cohesive Relations

In ideational structure, *cohesive relations* are established when a voter and a representative interpret an element in one proposition from a prior proposition because of the political relationship underlying them. The operative words here are *'cohesive'* and *'interpret.'* If either a representative interprets or a voter interprets, then an act of discovery in meaning is performed, which is conceived in light of individual beliefs, judgments, or circumstances. Since each individual is somewhat unique in his/her thinking and interpretation, the possible outcomes of any type or relations can be staggering to say the least. But in political behavior, there tends to be a group or collective consciousness rather than individual decisions floating aimlessly. Therefore, interpretation of cohesive relations becomes problematic when being reduced to an element in one or more propositions to the actual or perceived semantic word meanings. One method that is suggested to avoid this possible behavioral entanglement is *Semantic Representation With and Without Logic* (Abdul Karim Bangura 1994:153-161), which suggests a language model that uses contrasting approaches among logical techniques to reduce sense and reference meaning with those which use formal logic as a reductionist tool and as a representational form. It is virtually impossible for semantics to be absent from the cohesive relations. What does occur, however, is that cohesive relations raise the importance of language and communication used between voters and representatives.

It is the dominant ruling class that controls society by way or services, goods, and public safety. The propositions of the dominant ideology are what the people hear most of the time (I. Katznelson and M. Kesselman 1979:29). This dominant ideology is what Marx meant by the term *ruling ideas*. Put forth by established authorities, the propositions of the dominant ideology praise traditional arrangements, denies the existence of subordinates, and opposes political change. The dominant ideology makes alternatives to established arrangements appear risky and irresponsible and thus undercuts dissent (Katznelson and Kesselman 1979:23). Furthermore, in terms of cohesive relations, Katznelson and Kesselman describe three elements of the dominant ideology: (1) *Materialism, consumerism, and possessive individualism--capitalist values*, which are some of the key elements in the dominant ideology. Here is where a capitalist system legitimizes itself through the promise of material abundance; thus, the dominant ideology gains support and power through its promise of even greater wealth of material. This type of thinking is reinforced in the dominant group because for capitalists poverty scarcely exists. (2) *Procedural democracy and freedom*, which is the illusion that existing arrangements are democratically chosen when in fact the democratic process is confined to a very narrow decision--making process. (3) *Patriotism*, which helps to attain an almost religious intensity, along with national security, limits the criticism of existing arrangements. (4) *Technology* raises sophisticated and complex questions involved in keeping a great economic system going while it really acts as a ploy to reinforce dominant values of materialism (Katznelson and Kesselman 1979:30-32).

Public safety is listed separately because one of the primary objectives of the capitalist system is to protect the property and lives of the dominant ruling class. Thus, the language and the ideas necessarily follow this same pattern. Katznelson and Kesselman (1979:21) quote Karl Marx and Frederick Engels who said *"The ideas of the ruling class are in every epoch the ruling ideas....The class which has the means of material production at its disposal has control at the same time over the means of mental production."* In a cohesive relation setting, the dominant class or group exacts its meaning upon the ideas that proceed from the dominant group to the non-dominant group. It is at this point that negotiations for ideas, services, and goods initiate between the voters and representatives. The representative, needless to say, manipulates the outgoing idea so that every aspect of this idea best indulges his/her purpose. To the representative this political behavior is not seen as inappropriate or unethical, but it is communicated as networking, building coalitions or bonding with the public.

The result of this political behavior is division and conflict among constituent voters. According to E. E. Schattschneider (1960:650), it is impossible to keep the old and cultivate the new at the same time; people must choose among conflicts. In other words, conflicts compete with each other. Katznelson and Kesselman (1979:22-23) identify at least three separate groups that emerge out of conflict, *the dominant, the accommodationist, and the radical* (we have discussed the characteristics of the dominant group). The accommodationist group perceives a host of problems with the current system of government such as wages, poverty, unemployment, crime, poor health, sexual discrimination, excessive military spending, corruption, and high taxes. Furthermore, the accommodative ideology accepts the basic structure of inequality as natural and inevitable. The accommodative ideology seeks to improve these diverse areas. However, the accommodationist does not see these problems as collective, but separate, each requiring its own solution.

The radical group, on the other hand, refuses to define the problems of democracy in this way, but views them as systems of inequality in political and economic resources. The propositional ideology of the radical group historically links inequality and injustice in the United States, for example, to the tension between capitalist production and procedural democracy. Furthermore, for radicals, reforms should not be rejected out of hand, but neither should they be accepted uncritically. Reforms should be judged or evaluated as to whether they are broad contributions to mobilize significant change (Kaztnelson and Kesselman 1979:50-52).

Topic Relations

What are the issues or non-issues that are communicated among voters and representatives? Who generally initiates the communication transaction? Why do voters and representatives communicate at all? These questions are a few that emerge from the understanding that topic relations are concerned with the content of communication among voters and representatives.

It can be argued from the position of cohesive relations that the dominant class will invariably impose its ideology upon the minority class. What actually is proposed is, in fact, what the dominant class considers important enough to discuss. The dominant ideology is what people hear most of the time (Katznelson and Kesselman (1979:29). Therefore, existing economic and political arrangements frequently appear not merely as the best possible arrangements but as the only possible ones because of the power of the dominant ideology. This interpersonal communication, when discovered by the minority class, usually evokes antagonistic responses toward the dominant ideology. The responses from the minority class include (1) total submission to the dominant ideology on all political transactions, (2) collaboration of the voter and the representative to obtain a win-win situation on most political transactions, or (3) total opposition by both voter and representative on all political transactions.

Total submission to the dominant ideology is discussed in the section on Cohesive Relations. One can only add that the conversations for the most part will be controlled and dominated by the group that is in power at the time. The net result of this approach is that the poor are usually the victims of the dominant ideology (Michael Parenti 1974:158). The political significance of this type of dominance is low voter participation. The voters of this group are disproportionately concentrated among rural poor, the urban slum dwellers, the welfare recipients, the underemployed, the non-union workers, and the racial minorities. The entire voting process is dominated by middle-class styles and conditions which tend to discourage lower-class participation. The voters of this group tend to respond to propositions from an internal or external sense.

Secondly, according to Parenti (1974:165), the way people respond topically to political reality entirely depends upon collaboration of the voter and the representative to obtain a win-win situation on most political transactions. This reality is viewed in terms of how it is presented to them. Compromise among voters and representatives is generated in a win-win situation when, according to Parenti

Ideational Structure 85

(1974:144), the differences between the parties appear worrisome enough to induce many citizens to vote--if not *for* then *against* someone. While there is no great hope that the party of their choice will do much for them, there persists the fear that the other party, if allowed to take office, will make things even worse. This lesser-of-two-evils approach is perhaps the most important inducement to voter participation.

According to Charles Lindblom (1968:30), this level of topical relations produces the highest opportunity for policy-making. He states that *"policy can only be made through cooperation...."* Thus, the main content of this collaborative effort is concerned with policy-making and the giving and sharing of the power that it generates. Lindblom identifies three underlying mechanisms or processes in the play of power in policy making as follows (Lindblom 1968:30):

I. The play of power is a process of cooperation among specialists.

II. The play of power is not a substitute for policy analysis, simply resolving those issues left unsettled by analysis. Instead, policy analysis is incorporated as an instrument or weapon into the play of power, changing the character of analysis as a result.

III. The play of power proceeds, for the most part, according to rule; it is *'gamelike.'*

Although Lindblom calls the relation between power and policy *'gamelike,'* the communication among voters and representatives follow the rules of reasoning and critical thinking discussed earlier.

Parenti discusses a co-opted approach to compromise and cooperation, which is quite different from the approach discussed by Lindblom. This co-opted approach involves the use of money as a leverage to political stalemate or opposition. Because of this, it is no wonder that lower-status groups are skeptical that one candidate can change things. Their suspicions can be summarized as follows (Parenti 1974:160):

(1) the reform-minded candidate is still a politician and therefore is as deceptive as any other;

(2) even if he is sincere, the reformer is eventually *"bought off"* by

the powers that be;

(3) even if he is not bought, the reformer can do little against those who run things.

An example of this is a combination of a valid hypothetical syllogism and an invalid modus ponens. For example, Modus Ponens (**MP**) suggests:

(a) If the people want four more years of the same type of politics, then vote for Bill Clinton. The people want four more years of the same. Therefore, vote for Bill Clinton.

MP, by definition, is a valid syllogism; if we assume that the premises are true, it is impossible for the conclusion to be false. However, following Perenti's logic, given that Bill Clinton is considered a reformer catapulted in the midst of Reaganomics, Clinton still represents politicians and is deceptive as his associates. Therefore, in principle, the voter verbalizes (a) above; but internally, the voter is considering (a) above as a hypothetical syllogism. For example, Hypothetical Syllogism (**HP**) would suggest that

(b) If the people want four more years of the same type of politics, then vote for Bill Clinton. But if you vote for Bill Clinton, then be prepared to vote for another deceptive politician. So if the people want four more years of the same type of politics, then be prepared to vote for another deceptive politician. Assuming that the premises are true, again it is impossible for the conclusion to be false. Thus, (**HP**) could be the topic relation discussed among politicians who want certain voters to relinquish allegiance from one candidate or representative for another. Where (**MP**) represents the type of topic relation discussed among voters, the following example can be suggested:

(c) If voting for health care reform will change the standard of living, then the people of Washington, DC should register to vote. Voting for health care reform will change the standard of living. Therefore, the people of Washington, DC should register to vote.

The structures of these examples are consistent with the principles of reasoning established earlier. The voter and the representative may or may not know any of these principles; nevertheless, their initial conversations will crudely follow along the rules of reasoning with or without their knowing.

Functional Relations

What roles do ideas play in relation to one another and within the overall political context? The origin of an idea in the political context comes from the images that stimulate the sight. The object that stimulates sight creates the idea (Runes 1955:314-316). In the political context, ideas stimulate discussion, debate, and controversy. Therefore, ideas either originate in the course of a stimulating discussion, result from intense debate, or evolve from controversy.

What happens to ideas in politics depends upon the way people are divided into factions, parties, groups, classes, etc. Thus, ideas are divided along party lines, decided upon based on which group has more power than another, and sometimes ideas are created from conflict. These ideas are discussed to the extent that conflicts divide people and unite them at the same time, and the process of consolidation is as integral to conflict as the process of division. The more fully the conflicting idea is developed, the more intense it becomes, and the more complex is the consolidation of the opposing camps (Schattschneider 1960:62-63). Thus, it can be seen that ideas affect change. For instance, the idea that every American is entitled to adequate health care sparked a national debate on the issue. Eventually, ideas become policy, if enough political debate, discussion, and voter participation are wisely implemented in the process.

In **functional relations**, there is at least one faction or group established primarily within a political organization for the sole purpose of developing ideas to raise money and support the party. Money is not just one of many campaign resources, it is the *life blood* of electoral politics, helping to determine the availability of manpower, organization, tactical mobility, and media visibility. Without money, the politicians days are numbered (Parenti 1974:150). (The notion that money is a critical medium of exchange in a democratic political process is highlighted in chapter two.)

Conclusion

What we have attempted to demonstrate in this chapter is the importance of *ideational structure* in shaping political behavior. The significance of the discussion is that political life in a democratic society is highly impacted by those dominant ideologies that have been carefully strategized. Therefore, it behooves us to not only understand the strategies, but also to respond logically to the strategies.

When voters engage in either conversation, debate, argumentation or dialogue with representatives, they usually recognize a sense of dominance on the part of the representative. This interchange can proceed in one of many directions, depending on the level of sophistication of propositional logic used by either the voter or the representative. Either party may or may not be trained in this area, but their level of sophistication was gained perhaps through experience. Nevertheless, in a highly technological society where goods and services are in high demand, the individual or group with the deduction and inductive intellect can often gain significant ground in spite of the odds.

What voters think, feel, and do in politics arise out of their understanding or misunderstanding of the propositions presented. The voters who are inept at interpreting the complex propositional statements will always be dominated before and after the polls. It does not matter whether the propositions are associated with either *cohesive relations, topic relations, or functional relations.*

Propositions emerge out of ideas and very often in the midst of conflict. Thus, ideas and critical thinking are the well-spring for developing propositions. Once formulated, propositions may fall into several categories such as *internal sense, moral, external or empirical.* But, the main problem with the selection of propositions by the voters (i.e. citizens) is that they are generally based on morality. Quite often, the citizen presents an idea based on what 'ought' or 'should be the case,' instead of 'what is the case.' This approach often stymies the citizen, causing voter apathy and low turn-out at the polls.

Ideational Structure

Ideational structure is very important in a democratic society. The participation at this level by the voter is extremely important and is the basis for change in any democratic society. When representatives fail to fulfill their obligation to the public, then the accomodationist citizen, as well as the radical citizen, uses reason to asses their options. The freedom of a democratic society helps to incubate the propositions necessary for a change to take place. The merit of a proposition may be based or judged totally on its popularity, media coverage, or political timing in lieu of its actual value to the citizens. Some citizens may choose not to participate in politics as stated in *Information State* (refer to chapter six for more on this) by passively watching media devices, but in *Ideational Structure* this method serves as a means of informing and subconsciously involving an otherwise unreachable population. This group will almost always select moral propositions as its logical approach to democratic participation.

Finally, the function of *ideational structure* serves for some as the only means of political participation on any level. The candidates constantly focus on the middle-class for their elevation to political office. However, many grass-roots politicians recognize that the lower-class or marginalized citizen also wants to participate in the democratic process, but fails to become motivated in this area because of personal problems such as illiteracy, homelessness, poor health, transportation, joblessness, no political representation, no voting history, and lack of access to goods and services.

Chapter 5

Participation Framework

Introduction

A representative democracy is more than a structural polity. It should be viewed more appropriately as a description of the relationship between active citizens (i.e. voters) and their elected leaders (i.e. representatives). The relevancy of participation in a democracy is that representatives rationally take a cue from the active citizenry. Since our framework centers on the representative democratic model, we argue that voters and representatives understand the fundamental rules of the game (i.e. the primacy of electoral decisions). As a result, both actors possess precise expectations of the political system.

On the other hand, a somewhat compelling view of representative democracy is that on one level it can be interpreted to mean passivity and on another level it breeds passive citizenship (Glen Tinder 1993). This character is what Jean-Jacques Rousseau (1950) in particular criticized. Part of Rousseau's criticism about representative democracy centers around the perceived notion that "you are free when you vote but at other times you are a subject rather than a sovereign." The fact that representative democracy is accused of breeding passivity is somewhat of a truism. However, sustained and active participation is the apt prescription. The ability to transform a passive citizenry to become an active one is what qualifies a representative system as a system that deliberates on the entire political order of a polity's life. An active citizenry accepts the responsibility of having a partial sense of control over the polity. Arguably, such responsibility is more likely to be achieved when voters know the issues and know the candidates' positions. Inherent in a representative democracy is that every voter is attributed a region of responsibility. This responsibility dictates to the voter that by not participating, the average voter can be "squeezed" out by interest groups and other powerful socio-political groups. Finally, from the perspective of a representative democracy, the participatory logic may be described as an interactive process in which representatives articulate and influence voter opinions, while the electorate constitutes a responsible yet critical audience.

Studying Participation: A Behavioral Approach

The behavioral revolution in the study of politics has produced fascination with the activities of voters and their representative.[12] Their motivations are part of the transactions that take place between political actors in a representative democracy (Dougals Arnold 1990). In a representative democracy, the individual continues to retain the capacity for meaningful political action. Those in public life are more likely to be aware of and pay attention to the needs and preferences of those who are active. Sydney Verba et al (1993) point out that political leaders make promise to protect entitlement programs such as social security, veterans benefits, and medicare because of the relevant involvement of a sizeable amount of voters who care about these issues. On the other hand, representatives scarcely mention protecting programs of the marginalized, for example, food stamp, subsidized housing, or medicaid. The consequences of participation, and active participation in particular, are easily realized. We must point out that an active citizenry is not similar to an interest group. Thus, representatives who take into consideration the ideas of active groups do not necessarily pander to special interests. Activity in this instance is associated with participation, especially the political acts of voter mobilization and voting. In short, an active citizenry

---

[12]While the behavioral revolution in political science has been primarily an American phenomenon, it has had some consequences for research development in other democracies as well.

proposes and a responsible representative disposes (details on the act of voting appear in chapter three).

Individuals are active in the sense that they view voting as a mechanism that may produce change in the political system. Voting is an activity extremely germane to the general democratic logic. It is the one participatory act for which there is mandated equality (Verba et al 1993). This is true because in a democracy, each voter has one and one only legitimate vote.[13] Voters acting in unwitting orchestration can change the composition of the legislature, re-elect an incumbent legislator, or deluge the White House switchboard with telephone calls protesting a government's announced intentions on domestic and foreign policies.

The behavioral approach to political participation means focusing on how individuals act politically and seeking explanations for that behavior within those individuals. In our case, it also incorporates the relationships between voters and their representatives. Behavioralists espouse that representatives are sensitive not only to interest groups, but also to pressure from the voting public. Representatives must explain and justify their policy positions to the electorate by articulating a vision of public interest and showing how a proposed policy is logically connected to widely shared public values and motivations (Arnold 1990). The voting public needs to see a believable logic behind the program and policy stances of its representatives. In essence, the behavioralist approach to political participation concerns itself with what human beings do when they act politically--that is, when they vote, contact their representatives or articulate their political convictions.

The Rise of Behavioralism

The ready availability of aggregate voting statistics made for an early interest in participation, especially viewing elections as behavioral phenomena. Evidence of the increasing maturity of this

---

[13]Voting is one form of participation activity. Voter participation, especially those with tremendous impact on representation, include other activities such as contributing to a political campaign and letter writing to representatives.

research interest is the fact that scholars, using both aggregate statistics and survey data, have come to seek insight into, and test propositions about, macro aspects of the political process, such as the viability of political participation (Margaret Conway 1985).

Furthermore, behavioralist investigations of political participation range from the intensive study of images of political parties and candidates held by citizens to voters' orientations toward issues and involvement in the political process. In general, political behavior has moved from the preoccupation with electoral participation in the direction of discovering the relations taking place between voters and representatives. Attention has been moved away from the overt declarations of voters only to the circumstances that at any one time define the transaction between voters and representatives. The responsibilities of voters to representatives and vice-versa is now taking a central component of behavioral analysis. This transactions take into consideration the ability of voters to replace representatives and for representatives to act authoritatively in the allocation of values.

If the People Rule Indirectly, What is the nature of the Relationship between Voter and Representative?

Joseph Schumpeter (1943) makes a compelling case for politicians to compete for the people's vote. Given the broader implications of his analysis, one can see that competition for votes keep politicians interested in what voters have to say. Although voters might not be able to present a rational debate, they exert indirect pressure on the policy process and leadership. This pressure on leadership is what forces leadership to participate in reasonable debate over issues affecting the polity. Schumpeter contributes effectively to this notion of a realistic participatory role of the citizenry. For him, as we stated in chapter one, a representative democracy represents an "institutional arrangement for arriving at political decisions, in which prospective leaders acquire the power to decide by means of a competitive struggle for the people's vote" (1943:250). In Schumpeterian terms, the primary essence of a representative democratic system is that it allows people as a whole to have the "final word." This characteristic is the same, regardless of the democratic nature of the political system. Western European voters seem to reward parties and representatives who provide them with political leadership and a sense of ideological direction (Torben Iversen 1994). Characteristically, these voters, like all knowledgeable voters, punish politicians for being unresponsive to voter sentiments.

The continued importance of the voter in a representative framework can be interpreted as a consequence of the primacy of the "vote." Voting is central to the democratic method because it provides the mechanism through which the influencing of leadership can take place. The representative modality is concerned with processes by which ordinary citizens exert a relatively high degree of indirect influence over leaders. The ability to vote for leaders empowers the voting public. This characteristic is not singular to the voting public. A representative democratic system also empowers those who are intelligent, politically experienced, and those who have concern for political and social concerns. These individuals are empowered with the responsibility of leadership. Representatives, acting as leaders, provide better opportunities for a well-administered political system. This is a serious shortcoming when one considers the practicality of a direct democratic system.

Schumpeter (1943) criticizes direct democracy for its idealistic belief in the "people" directly managing the political framework. His rationale reiterates the impossibility associated with the notion of the "people" having to hold definite positions on all questions confronting the polity. For Schumpeter, relegating authority to a representative eliminates the problems that voters might experience with complicated affairs of the state. He reiterates this point by indicating that "it is leaders who must be active, initiate and decide" (1943:283). In essence, Schumpeter's reconceptualized analysis altered the notion of representation found in the democratic model. In addition, it is against this background that Schumpeter's alternative stresses the bargaining power and utility of the vote and voter participation.

Interrelationship Between Voters and Representatives

At this point, one can clearly see that linkages between voters and their representatives constitute the truest form of democratic theory. The notion of the constituencies having an influence on their representatives is core to the representative logic. Such a logic comports well with the rationality of an existing legislature. For instance, in the United States Congress, the perceived wisdom has long held that constituency preferences influence many aspects of congressional behavior (Morris Fiorina 1977). This whole idea of a relevant constituency gains overwhelming significance in situations where the voting public is a deprived public (John Gaventa 1982). Deprivation can come in the form of political atomization or economic marginalization. The relevancy of this situation is that, in theory, in a representative democracy voting in elections is a principal way for deprived entities to act upon their concerns. It is assumed that the potential issue affecting the deprived public would coalesce with the position of the representatives. The electorate would, it is hoped, reject representatives who do not affirm voters' positions in their own policy pronouncements. Representation of disadvantaged groups, particularly by members (i.e. "one of their own") of these groups, must be encouraged because at times the desires and wants of disadvantaged groups are manipulated by the mainstream political class through appeals to mainstream symbols, thereby leading to quiescence. The rationalization here is that a deprived public would vote for individuals promoting the welfare of the group. Furthermore, disadvantaged groups in a democratic system are free and constitutionally bounded to take actions upon their concerns.

There are inordinate ways polities structure the interaction between their citizens and their representative leaders. The relationship between voters and representative leaders is one that inculcates an element of linkage. In light of our framework, linkage is used in this context to refer to the way the general public (i.e. voters) connects with the leaders who make policy decisions. This definition places appropriate emphasis on the connection between one political unit and another in terms of the way decisions made at one level (e.g., decisions made by voters) influence those made at another level (e.g., decisions made by elected officials).

Voter-Representative Linkages in Democratic Politics

This type of linkage is present when there is some way to ensure that leadership decisions will be responsive to the views of the ordinary voters, albeit not made by them. In this manner citizens continuously have a form of indirect access to public policy, while exerting direct pressure on the representative at election time and also through their tenure (Larry Bartel 1991). This is the essence of a representative government. This political framework emphasizes that ordinary citizens choose government to carry out their political aspirations and wishes. The citizenry plays a central role in emphasizing this linkage. The reason for this is that citizens must take account of the public policy stands of candidates when they cast their votes.

Robert Weissberg (1978:536) indicates that "representation means a high correlation between constituency opinion and roll-call voting on a pair-wise basis." In such a system, more emphasis is placed on the electorate to replace representatives who show signs not compatible with the spirit of the citizenry. In other words, participation can be viewed as a mechanism that might produce alternative leaders. Obviously, both the representative and participative loci occur in their truest forms when the representatives are clearly chosen and removed from office at least partially on the basis of their stands on issues affecting the voters.

It is our purpose to further the research that emphasizes reciprocal political relationships between voters and representatives. Thus, policy distances may be consequences as well as causes of voter preference. This is a very important premise because the fact remains that many voters complain about the detachment of representatives from their daily lives. The fact also remains, however, that Americans, for example, now feel notably dissatisfied with their representatives and their primary public institutions. For example, a Times Mirror Center for the People and the Press report (1994) recently provided concrete evidence of voters changing their attitudes toward government and politicians. The survey indicates that when asked whether most elected officials care about what ordinary people think, just 33 percent of the respondents said they do, compared with 47 percent in the 1987 Times Mirror poll. The citizenry's general attitudes toward America's basic democratic ideals continue to be challenged. Such challenges in the form of negative judgements have been intensifying. The proportion of voters who continue to indicate that the American government is not run for the benefit of all climbed from 39 percent in 1987 to 57 percent in 1994 (Times Mirror 1994).

A noteworthy conclusion from the aforementioned study does affirm our confidence on the representative system generally. There is a tendency to assume that this dissatisfaction with politics and politicians is part of a more general psychological unrest--a loss of confidence in the democratic institutions and the logic of our representative system. However, the Times Mirror evidence indicates that about 68 percent of the respondents agreed that the system will always find a way to solve problems. One can conclude that such a response is indeed a tacit approval of the democratic theory and representative logic.

Another way of looking at the general conclusions from the Times Mirror report is that, generally, voters in a representative democracy are not besieged by comprehensive political malaise. What they are usually calling for are choices reflecting their demands before they agree to support politicians or new initiatives. This dissatisfaction, coming in the face of the progress of the representative system, seems to result in large measure from a breakdown in the mechanism (i.e. voting) designated to translate public expectations and choices into public policy. This diminished public satisfaction with the polity is buttressed by a continuing problem the citizenry has with the notion of "representativeness." The latter revolves around the fact that voters have questions concerning the extent to which representatives in legislative bodies actually represent their constituents.

Partisan factors, ideological principles, and complex issues concerning the intensity of interest groups convolute the process which determines whether a representative has represented his/her constituents in a given situation. For example, did representatives vote in the manner that their constituents wanted them to vote for the North American Free Trade Association (NAFTA) legislation in 1994? The perception that representatives are "out of touch" with their constituencies produces caustic reaction on the part of voters towards their representatives. On the other hand, it must be pointed out that part of the representative logic is that representatives should use their own judgement as well as reflect public interest and opinion. The verdict is still out on the issue of what kind of representatives citizens of a representative democracy want. Do citizens of representative democracies want representatives who espouse representing the country and its people or representatives who espouse focusing on the constituencies that elected them? (Weissberg 1978).

Views on Representation

If constituency service carries with it nothing but benefits for most members of the legislature, the function of representation is less certain and even carries with it some danger that the legislator will lose his/her bid for re-election. Generally, representation means that the many competing interests in society should be represented in the legislature. There are at least two major views on representation, a brief discussion of which follows.

1. The Trustee View of Representation

In answering the question how is representation to be achieved, the *trustee view* approach suggests that legislators act as trustees of the broad interest of the entire society. In other words, they should vote against the narrow interests of their constituents as their conscience and perceptions of national needs dictate (Weissberg 1978).

2. The Instructed-Delegate View of Representation

Directly opposed to the trustee view of representation is the instructed-delegate view: the notion that the members of the legislature should behave as instructed delegates. Put differently, they should mirror the views of the majority of the constituents who elected them to power in the first place (Weissberg 1978).

Anti-Representation: Voter Anger and Frustration

It is apparent that in a representative democracy, voters' problems concerning perceived political immobility fall on the shoulders of elected officials. This means that more than likely voters associate and link political inertia to the fact that their representatives are not performing their assigned responsibilities. For instance, citizens may complain that taxes are too high, that the government intrudes too much, and that the government wastes money. The general perception among citizens is that policy deficiencies are a result of ineffective leadership. Most of the discontent reflects a questioning of political leadership more than the institutions of government. Understandably, political atomization of the citizenry produces critical comments and assessments. It is not uncommon to hear voters make statements such as "politicians have been in the legislature for years and have not accomplished much." Voter antagonism is manifested in overt statements because it is difficult for voters to evaluate their representatives on the basis of actual or perceived performance. Incumbent politicians in particular feel the wrath of voters who perceive themselves to be peripheral to the decision-making mechanism. Therefore, the systemic problems of unemployment, inflation, and higher taxation are interpreted as manifestations representative of neglected promises.

In a representative democracy, representatives are held responsible for the efficacy of the system and public policy. Poor national economic performance may be beyond the realm of representative control. In reality, such a situation may have been brought about due to decades of government neglect. Despite the fact that policy problems might be a result of the governmental engine, the citizenry is usually not willing to accept structural and exogenous factors as primary contributory factors. In such an environment, the solutions proposed by representatives are considered not more than rhetoric containing nothing new, substantial, or innovative. This is unfortunate in that voters have short memories and no patience with bureaucratic details.

As a result, elected leaders of a representative framework have the responsibility of arousing the motivation and values of the voters. In a democracy in particular, it is not sufficient for leadership to merely exercise power; the mobilization of the followers (i.e. voters) toward an end is also important. Hence, a central premise to the representative theory is that true choices (i.e. elected leaders) of the people cannot wield power without paying attention to the goals and needs of the citizenry. The coalescence of goals and needs by both voters and representatives is a mark of shared motives and linkages. To represent someone, one must induce followers to "act for certain goals that represent the values and motivations...of both leaders and followers" (James Macgregor Burns 1978:19).

The coalescence of the rules of the game and the values of the system all point toward the issue of having a consensus between voters and representatives. Some theorists have taken a comprehensive view of the utility of consensus in a democratic framework. Bernard Berelson et al (1954) indicate that for a political democracy to survive, a basic consensus must bind together the contending parties. In this book, we submit the position that agreement on the common fundamentals of a representative democracy is essential between voters and representatives. At the broadest level, the most important agreement should emphasize the common desire to operate an effective democratic system. Hence, we are speaking of general commitments to procedures necessary for the implementation of a representative system, the acceptance of governing principles such as majority rule and minority rights, public officials should be chosen by majority vote, and citizens should have an equal chance to influence governmental policies.

The relationship that emerges between voters and representatives is based on both entities fulfilling basic responsibilities. Thus, when voters inevitably complain about the system, they should investigate their frustration deeper; it may reveal less than glaring democratic commitments and responsibilities on their part. In the politically unsettled American political environment of 1992, for example, Democratic Senator Jay Rockefeller of West Virginia, commenting on the relationship of voters and their representatives, indicated that "voters are angry with politicians like me and they are angry with you in the media...well let me tell you something, the voters are no bargain either." If the senator is right, what then is lacking in voters' responsibilities? What are the things that the voters should be doing that they are not doing? First and foremost, the voters, it seems, often are of two minds, and sometimes three, or more. This means that when it comes to the expectations of their representatives, on the one hand, and the overall governmental approach, on the other hand, the political minds of citizens are usually not clearly made up. For instance, voters fiercely demand that Congress end "pork-barrel" projects, but not the projects located in their districts. The same applies to the call for reducing federal spending. Again, voters consistently want to keep those spendings that benefit their jurisdictions.[14]

American voters seem convinced that Congress does nothing at all, but voters also remain hugely unaware of the on-goings of the legislature. Voters are definitely clueless about major legislative successes. Likewise, most voters are largely clueless about how their candidates or representatives stand on major issues. What is even more disturbing is the distance that exists between voters and representatives about what the nature of representation should be. Furthermore, voters often accuse representatives of being parochial and lack a "big picture" national perspective. Representatives are often accused of solely being interested in getting re-elected. However, a September 1994 ABC poll indicated otherwise (*The Washington Post* 1994). When asked what they wanted their representatives to do, the responses were the complete opposite to some generally held beliefs. A total of 58 percent of Americans indicated that their representatives should try to direct more government spending to their respective districts. As a corollary, 73 percent of Americans indicated that representatives should be trying to bring federal projects to their district; a total of 90 percent indicated that representatives should be attempting to help create jobs in the district. One conclusion that can be drawn from these results is that the resigned voter disillusionment may be partially imbedded in a lack of knowledge of the political system. It seems that voters have declared war against representatives and representation; however, voters are violating the golden rule about engagement, which is "know thy enemy." There is a disparity between the role of voters in a democracy and what voters actually want.

Factors Influencing Political Participation

The presence of external forces exerting influence on voters as well as on representatives is a common characteristics of 20th century

---

[14]Pork-barrel is considered to be favoritism by legislators in the allocation of benefits or resources. It also involves legislation that favors the district of a particular legislator by providing for the funding of public works or other projects (such as post offices or defense contracts) that will bring economic advantage to the district and political favor for the legislator.

representative democracies. This, more than anything else, is the contemporary theme in the politics of representation. The influences of recognizable political actors on voters must therefore be assessed. The case with most representative democracies is that the role of groups is secondarily acknowledged; however, the doctrine of the individual voter's supremacy is still invoked. In practice though, the representatives and the policies they implement are influenced and even determined by well-organized political actors. Far from being cynical, one notices that no matter which representatives are in office, there are pressures for continuity of government policies rather than genuine calls for change.

This section concerns itself with factors influencing participation (i.e. mobilizing agents) in general and does not take into consideration the reasons why mobilizing institutions have failed to an extent to increase participation. The latter continues to gain research interest in the United States because compared to other representative democracies, the United States is distinguished by its relatively low level of voter turn-out (Walter Burnham 1982).

Political Parties

In a representative democracy, the role of political parties in mobilizing political participation is of major concern. Political parties have and continue to play a central role in increasing participation by the electorate (Samuel Eldersweld 1982). E. E. Schattschneider's position seems to support this thesis when he indicates that

> the rise of political parties is arguably one of the principal distinguishing marks of modern government. The parties, in fact, have played a major role as makers of government, more especially they have been the makers of democratic governments (1942:1).

In spite of the fact that the United States, for example, is essentially a candidate-centered political system, political parties play a vital role in political mobilization. In other parts of the democratic world, especially in Western Europe, parties really do matter when it comes to political participation and mobilization. In Western European representative systems, democracy essentially means party politics. In essence, the party will continue its role as a crucial mobilization actor.

In order to see how political parties affect general participation, we must answer the following question: What are political parties and how do they contribute to participation? Political parties consist of groups of individuals with the same common ideas about government. The main purpose of political parties is to manage and control governments (see chapter six for a discussion of the instruments used toward this end). However, a political party is a multi-faceted political structure. It could mean several things to various individuals in or out of the party. Frank Sorauf (1967:37-58) conceives of political parties as existing in three arenas. First, the political party exists as an organization in which citizens with the same political ideas join for concerted actions to achieve political, social, and economic goals. Second, the party exists in the form of political offices; that is, party members are part of the legislature. Finally, the party exists in the form of an electorate which, though the least stable and least well-organized of the three arenas, is composed of those citizens who have a psycho-cultural connection to the party label and who generally show support for it at the polls. The crucial question then is this: How does the party, giving its utility, produce participation among voters? Our concern here is that the crucial relationship that ensues is one where the political party, constituting officeholders and activists, on the one hand, influence the electorate, on the other. This state of affairs is crucial not only for party development, but also because it is at this level that "getting the vote" is accomplished.

One of the primary roles ascribed to parties is the mobilization of voters to vote for respective party-supported candidates. It is clear that the origin and development of political parties is intimately connected with the increase in voter participation and the proliferation of elections. Hence, the development of political parties reflects the participatory imperative. The reasoning is clear because the democratic logic presupposes a degree of citizen participation and choice. Consequently, in order to bring about citizen participation, organizational intermediaries (i.e. political parties) also expand on their mobilizing functions.

In the United States and in most of the Western European democracies, as the electorates expanded, the parties also expanded their organizational forms to include more activists and mass memberships. The reality here is that parties dominated the socialization of new electorates (Sorauf 1982:441). These emerging electorates are marked with low levels of political information and sophistication. Hence, in this instance political parties contribute to participation by becoming the "chief givers of political cues" (Sorauf 1982:441). There are natural directional phases in the politicalization of the citizenry. The directional patterns invariably appear to be almost in one direction. The citizenry, due to the activities of political parties, progresses from lesser to greater politicalization. This, in turn, also dictates more and larger democracies and participatory expectations.

Another way political parties contribute to participation relates to them reducing the cost of having a democratic political system. There are economic costs associated with the interrelationship between the electorate and the government (see chapter six for details). Voters need to have a certain kind of information regarding governmental actions; and in a democratic system, it is part of the structural arrangement for the government to inform the electorate. These activities on the part of the government require resources; and if left by themselves, voters would find it exorbitant to gather all necessary information pertaining to electoral involvement. Thomas Palfrey and Howard Rosenthal (1985) have articulated the high cost inherent with democratic participation. They seem to concur with the position that the costs associated with articulating the democratic framework are high, in fact almost insurmountable if voters do not get external subsidy. Hence, political parties are indeed a way of reducing the transaction costs associated with political participation (Peter Wielhouser 1993).

The main logic in this section suggests that in order to vote, individuals have a decision to make and must acquire the minimal amount of information that enables them to act. However, since all information is costly, political parties provide indirect subsidies to voters to overcome the barriers to political information.

Interest Groups

Interest groups are another significant mobilizing agent that influence political participation.[15] The interest group logic espouses that individuals function primarily through groups and that these groups act as appropriate and necessary conduits to further group goals, which are based on common interests (Gregor Caldeira et al 1990). Hence, interest groups are political units organized to advance the causes of private and public organizations. Interest groups arise as a result of a common interest among certain individuals. It is often argued that interest groups are formed because citizens or corporations who are experiencing some form of deprivation or frustration want political redress. Threat to their existence prompts individuals or corporations to interact and become increasingly aware of their shared interests. As this growing awareness becomes intense, it stimulates vigilance and, more often than not, results in individuals or organizations forming an association to serve as their representative.

After being formed, one of the primary purposes of interest groups is to influence public opinion, the legislative system, and the overall polity. In trying to influence the polity, interest groups activate political participation. In this regard, interest groups espouse the idea that many citizens may and will vote in elections if they are well informed. Labor unions, for example, are typical interests groups constantly interacting and exerting legitimate influence on both the legislature and the overall polity. Labor's political power can influence its members to become active during elections. There is evidence that high voting turn-out is associated with individuals who are highly unionized (Robert Jackman 1987). Interest groups, such as labor, are able to marshall their members and sympathizers because they have a self-interest (e.g., keeping exports out) in influencing the political system. How their interests are pursued by representatives will depend importantly on how well they mobilize voters to vote for candidates with pro-labor political stances.

Interest groups induce mobilization through more than just supporting candidates. For instance, the American Association of

---

[15]One of the first specific references to groups in the American political process was James Madison's famous discussion of factions in Federalist Number 10.

Retired Persons (AARP) is now an important voice in any American dialogue that has repercussions on the aged. This group has been known to mobilize retirees toward a particular candidate or inform retirees about a particular domestic policy that may affect them directly, for example, the establishment of a national health care system.

An interest group's influence on mobilization is due in large part to how effective it is in politically stimulating individuals to come out and vote. Labor's rationale, for example, is this: With the availability of necessary political information, lower income individuals in particular should become more aware of their particular opportunity and vote. In the same context of trying to induce voters, certain groups take on a defensive political posture. For example, the American Medical Association (AMA) utilizes defensive efforts to ward-off potential citizenry and legislative gains by the Clinton Administration on the national health care system dialogue. The AMA information strategy centers on the position that citizens might lose certain medical benefits, if the existing system of health and medical care is replaced.

Conclusion

What then does all this tell us about the special relationship between voters and representatives? One thing we can say is that for the representative framework to be visualized, the political disposition of the masses is a crucial ingredient. The representative logic, and indeed all political loci, is built upon the capabilities and disposition of individuals. In the representative democratic modality, the voter embodies this disposition. On the other hand, the absence of specific political responsibilities and certain degree of mass voter approval, and representative prerogative and authority undermines the representative model of democracy.

In terms of political mobilization, political parties, the dominant vehicle for change in representative democracies, continue and more than likely will continue to be the strongest mobilizing agent. The reason for this is that political values that are formed and forged when a group of voters is newly enfranchised are strong and enduring. What this suggests is that subsequent political mobilization attempts involving winning the support of voters who are already aligned in terms of party and ideology become extremely difficult. This is probably the primary contributory factor regarding the "freezing" of mobilization efforts in the United States. Hence, there is a serious need for structural changes within the major political parties. One feature that will remain constant is the role of parties to provide information to an ever-demanding electorate. Political parties have had to subsidize the cost of information partly because voters are assumed to know the platform of the parties and to understand that a true representative government will result from bargaining (i.e. active participation) in the electoral process.

Chapter 6

Information State

Introduction

"*Information*," according to Anthony Downs (1957:79), "is data about current developments in and status of those variables which are the objects of contextual knowledge." Therefore, Downs proposes (a) without contextual knowledge, a person cannot interpret information; (b) an informed citizen is one with both contextual knowledge and information about those areas necessary for him/her to make decisions.

Thus, the study of information state in a democratic society is important because adequate information for the electorate is a precondition for any kind of action--electoral or demonstrative--to effect national policy. Furthermore, the distribution of information to the public is a function of wealth and power. Even the government can color citizens' understanding of events by its control of news at the source: press conferences, "leaks"[16] to the press, White Papers, and "truth experts" going around the country at taxpayers' expense. In the case of private media, the large networks and mass-circulation newspapers and magazines have the greatest access to citizens' minds.

---

[16]"Leaks" are planted stories used by government information providers for either supporting or opposing a public policy. A typology of leaks will be discussed later in this chapter.

There is no "equal time" for critics of public policy to present their views.

The discussion of the political context of information state, as it relates to political behavior, can be segmented into at least five interrelated areas: (1) acquiring and selecting information, (2) providers and availability of information, (3) uses of information, (4) costs of information, and (5) benefits of information. As the following discussion reveals, some of these areas have received relatively more attention than others.

Acquiring and Selecting Information

Some individuals acquire information as an end in itself. These individuals derive enjoyment from knowing that American talk-show host Oprah Winfrey has lost plenty of weight and kept it off, or that Brazil won the 1994 world football (soccer) championship. All such information obtained solely for the edification it provides is called "entertainment information" (Downs 1957:215) or "infotainment" (Thomas Dye, Harmon Zeigler, and S. Robert Lichter 1992:20), despite the seriousness of its content. Such information is dramatic or sensational presentations of news stories. The popular "60 Minutes" on CBS television and "20/20" on ABC television in the United States are leading illustrations of infotainment. On these shows, the key decisions about what will be said, when, and how are made by the executive producers. The criteria employed by these executive producers for selecting news are emotional and not intellectual. For example, a CBS executive producer, Don Hewitt, when asked for an explanation of his choices for stories, he replied:

> It's all instinctive....I'm the least intellectual person I know. A lot of times I say to a producer, I see it and I hear it but I don't feel it in the pit of my stomach. I don't make decisions intellectually. I make them viscerally. When I get bored, I figure other people will get bored. I have the ability to put myself in the place of the viewer because I have the same short attention span he has (quoted in Dye, Zeigler, and Lichter 1992:21).

Of course, not too many newspeople are as candid as Hewitt. He admits that the news he selects must be emotional, sensational, and satisfy people with short attention span.

Nonetheless, most information is employed as a means for decision-making. As with every means, the usefulness of such information and the manner in which it is selected hinge upon the desired end. As Downs (1957:215) suggests, any non-entertainment information can be classified into one of three categories, depending on how it is used: (1) *production information* for production decisions, (2) *consumption information* for consumption decisions, and (3) *political information* for political decisions.

For all three types of decision-making, Downs maintains, the basic rule for deciding how many data to obtain is the same. The voter or representative seeking information will invest resources to acquire data until the marginal return (the effects of net additions from the current conditions) from information equals its marginal cost (the effects of net subtractions from the current conditions). It is at this point, Downs adds, assuming decreasing marginal returns or increasing marginal costs or both, that the voter or representative would have enough information to make his/her decision (Downs 1957:215).

Subsequently, it is presupposed that the decision-maker already has a certain minimum of information in order to make decisions. S/he must, at the very least, realize that s/he has a decision to make and be aware of its general context. Thus, for the voter to make a voting decision, s/he must obtain information about the date of the election, the voting procedure, the number of contestants, the contestants' names, etc. In a democratic society, the continuous stream of free information present will give the voter this minimum before s/he starts calculating how much information to obtain (Downs 1957:215).

As Downs (1957:215-216) points out, three factors determine the size of a voter's planned information investment. The first is the value to the voter of making a correct decision as opposed to making an incorrect one, i.e. the variation in utility incomes (the benefit or satisfaction expected from a choice or course of action) associated with the possible outcomes of his/her decision. The second is the relevance of the information to the voter's decision. Questions such as "Is acquisition of this particular bit[17] of knowledge likely to influence the decision one way or another?" "If so, how likely?" are relevant here. To respond to these questions, a probability estimate of the chances that any given bit of information will alter the voter's decision is called for. This probability is then applied to the value of the voter making the right choice. From this calculation, an analyst can then estimate the return from the bit of information being considered, i.e. the voter's marginal return from investment in data on this particular margin. The third is the cost of the data. The marginal cost of any bit of information comprises the returns given up in acquiring it. To obtain any bit of information calls for the comparison of its estimated marginal cost and estimated marginal return. To determine the data to be acquired then requires comparisons for all bits.

According to Dye, Zeigler, and Lichter (1992:21), politics involves both entertainment and serious decision-making. Politics involves talk, expression, image, and picture--it involves drama and emotion. Politics also involves the struggle over allocating those things valued by citizens. It involves lobbying, pressuring, threatening, bargaining, and compromising; politics is indeed serious and significant. Politics involves vital decisions that affect us all--for example, whether to institute a national health program that will cover every American. Politics also involves the creation of images--for example, the image of Jimmy carter as champion of peace, the poor, and working persons.

If we lived in a perfectly informed world, information will be available to every decision-maker in unlimited amounts at no cost, and s/he will not need to consume time using that information. Consequently, the problem of selecting the most relevant information will not arise. But in the real world, as Downs observes, no matter how many data are available, the amount a rational decision-maker can use for any one decision is strictly limited for two reasons:

---

[17]*A **bit*** is the amount of information in a message that tells which of two equally likely events has taken place. For example, the part of the election result which tells the winner is Candidate Do Little contains **one bit** of information.

(1) the human mind, even when abetted by calculating machines, can encompass only a limited amount of information at once, and (2) assimilating and evaluating data take time, which is especially scarce in decision-making because of the pressure of events (Downs 1957:211).

These conditions, according to Downs, impose the necessity of selection upon a decision-maker, who must make choices from the vast supply of data available only a limited number to employ in his/her decisions. In addition, as Downs points out, there are costs associated with obtaining or using information besides the time involved. This fact, according to him, increases the pressure upon a decision-maker to reduce the number of data s/he uses. Since this pressure exists throughout the decision-making process, Downs maintains that an economic problem emerges at each of the aforementioned steps: "how much information (including judgments) should be sent to the next step?" (Downs 1957:211).

Downs further suggests that the basic economic nature of becoming informed necessitates the selection among data. What immediately arises is the crucial question of how to decide which data to select and which to reject. The importance of this question hinges on the fact that whatever answer is chosen determines what type of information is to be utilized in making decisions and thus shapes the decisions and their effectiveness. Furthermore, Downs reminds us, selection is not limited solely to the decision-maker and whoever does the selection has a potentially enormous influence upon decisions, even if s/he does not make them him-/her-self (Downs 1957:211).

Thus, all information used by the voter or the representative is by nature biased, since it is a selection of data from the vast amount extant, others of which could have as well been chosen. As Karl Mannheim (1955:93-94) succinctly puts it:

> History as history is unintelligible unless certain of its aspects are emphasized in contrast to others. This selection and accentuation of certain aspects of historical totality may be regarded as the first step in the direction which ultimately leads to an evaluative procedure and to ontological judgments (also quoted in Downs 1957:212).

Mannheim's statement is quite relevant to the process of the voter or the representative becoming informed, which has as its end the evaluative procedure of making decisions. Since evaluation begins with the selection of certain data as opposed to others, all such selection is relatively evaluative. In essence, no such thing exists as purely objective reporting of an event or a situation.

Every rational voter or representative then, following Downs, eventually constructs for his/her political consumption a system of information acquisition. This system has a limited number of information sources, a part of whose data output s/he selects to utilize in political decision-making. S/he has to rely on a rather crude process of trial and error experimentation to construct this system. If the system were to emerge as a truly rational one for the decision-maker, it will have to possess the following characteristics, according to Downs (1957:218):

> 1. The data reporters in it use principles of selection as nearly identical to his own as possible.
>
> 2. It is broad enough to report anything of significance in the differential areas, yet narrow enough to cull out data not worth knowing about. In short, it focuses his attention on facts germane to his decision-making.
>
> 3. It provides him with enough information about each issue for his decisions, given his desire to invest in information.
>
> 4. It has sufficient internal plurality so that its parts can be used as checks upon each other's accuracy and deviation from his own selection principles. To be effective as mutual checks, information sources must be independent as well as nominally separate; e.g., a radio station and a newspaper which both use only Associated Press reports do not really check each other.

Thus, Downs (1957:218) adds, the creation and maintenance of such a rational information system means that scarce resources will have to be absorbed, the cost of which must be balanced against the returns from the information acquired. In essence, the extent of a voter's or representative's rational information system depends greatly on the nature of the returns from the information.

Providers and Availability of Information

In every society, citizens are supplied with a constant flow of free information[18] on various subjects. The human being's psychological roots in his/her inquisitiveness, need for personal relationships with others, face-to-face contacts, need for close personal cooperation in production, leisure activities, rearing of children, and political action facilitate such free flow of information. The breadth of topics covered by this stream of free information varies from culture to culture and from person to person. In democratic societies, there is no ban on the free circulation of political data. According to Downs, citizens in a democratic society normally receive free political information in the following ways (1957:222-223):

1. The governing party publishes large amounts of information as an intrinsic part of its governing activities.

2. All political parties, including the one in power, put out partisan information for the purpose of influencing voters.

3. Professional publishers distribute some information that is wholly subsidized by advertisers (e.g., throwaways, television programs).

4. Interest groups publish information gratuitously in order to persuade citizens to accept their viewpoints.

5. Other private citizens provide free data in the form of letters, conversations, discussion groups, speeches, etc.

6. Entertainment sources sometimes yield political information as a surplus benefit from what is intended as an entertainment investment

---

[18]The notion of free information, as used here, refers to information given to a citizen without any transferable cost. The only cost s/he bears is the time s/he spends absorbing and using it. This definition is of course restrictive because none of the information a person receives is completely costless. Merely perceiving information requires time; and if a person assimilates it or thinks about it, these acts require more time. Unless the opportunity cost (i.e. the highest valued benefit that must be sacrificed or forgone as the result of choosing an alternative) is zero, which is unlikely, s/he must forgo a scarce resource to obtain that information.

(e.g., the newsreel in a motion picture theater). Some citizens also seek straight political information purely for its entertainment value because they enjoy political rivalry and warfare. Any strictly political values they get are consumer-surplus byproducts of the entertainment.

7. Similarly, information acquired in the course of making production or consumption decisions may have political value. Since this value is incidental to the purpose for which the data (are) obtained, it can be regarded as a free benefit.

Free political information from these sources, suggests Downs (1957:223), are of two types: (1) *accidental* data are by-products of the non-political activities of a citizen in that they accrue to him/her without any effort on his/her part to acquire them; (2) *sought-for* data, by implication, are those which accrue to a citizen when s/he makes special effort to find them. Thus, as Downs points out, the cost of accidental data is ordinarily much lower compared to that of sought-for data. According to him, the preceding sources (5), (6), and (7) yield mainly accidental data; whereas data from sources (2), (3), and (4) are usually ignored by citizens unless they are specifically looking for political information. Source (1), he adds, produces both accidental and sought-for types of data.

As Downs (1957:223) also notes, not all citizens receive the same amount of free data. Any citizen with time to spare can obtain a great deal of sought-for data, but variations in the quantity of accidental data received can result from several other factors as well. Indeed, the distribution of political power in a democracy may be strongly influenced by systematic variations in the amount of free information received and the ability to assimilate it.

It is obvious, therefore, that political decision-making in a large-sized democracy cannot be undertaken without exorbitant costs, unless (a) information is gathered by a few specialists for the many decision-makers and (b) the information an individual gets is prefocused upon the differential areas of decision. If both of these conditions are absent, individuals cannot begin reducing their personal data costs to match their personal returns from information (Downs 1957:225).

In most modern democracies, the division of labor determines who performs the role of information-provider. Specialization in procuring information facilitates the reduction of the per unit cost of data, making it possible for citizens to obtain information--though usually with subsidy. The problem of focusing attention is also solved by selecting for presentation only data within the differential areas. Besides private persons, there are four major types of information-providers upon whom decision-makers depend (Downs 1957:225-227). Each of these four is discussed separately.

1. Professional Data-Gatherers and Publishers

In their pursuit of profits, professional data-gatherers transmit only differential area information because that is what the consumers want. By its very name, "news" implies changes in the situation worth knowing about. The fact that publishers focus on the kind of data consumers want does not mean they always use the political selection principles consumers want. Publishers do relieve consumers of the overwhelming burden of surveying everything before picking out the few things that are sufficiently relevant to merit consideration.

2. Interest Groups

Interest groups usually focus their information output upon policies that seem about to change because their primary concern is influencing current government policy. Interest groups do this whether they favor or oppose changing these policies. They find it prudent, therefore, not to waste their resources publicizing 'dead' issues. Instead, they concentrate upon the very items that are most relevant to citizens' political decision-making. There are, of course, exceptions to this rule. It is true, however, that most data disseminated by interest groups are about events in the differential areas, partly because the agitation of such groups helps decide what matters lie within those areas.

3. Political Parties

The first thing on the list of every political party's goals is the winning of elections. Because this objective is relevant to political decision-making, all the information a political party issues bears upon this objective. Indeed, every party occasionally passes out irrelevant data as a deliberate smoke screen to cover up unfavorable facts or to increase the ambiguity of its positions on certain issues. In addition, every party traditionally produces a large output of sanctimonious platitudes praising the flag, motherhood, the home, military personnel, etc. So in order to emphasize those elements from which party differentials are formed, most of every party's emanations are either attacks on its opponents or defense of itself.

4. The Government

In addition to the usual information it puts out as a political party, a government also distributes large quantities of data as an intrinsic part of governing. Such data include administrative directives, new laws, research findings, and other notices given to citizens in the course of its operations. The production of a vast majority of these data is inspired solely by the necessities of administration and these data are not political in nature. Because these data tell citizens what policies the government is carrying out, they provide important evidence for citizens who make political decisions. A great deal of this information is therefore focused upon differential areas of action, since any changes in policy must be especially well-girded with instructions to those affected.

A crucial aspect about a government's role in providing information in a democracy is that it cannot force people to become well-informed for the following reasons (Downs 1957:247):

1. There is no reliable, objective, inexpensive way to measure how well-informed a (citizen) is.

2. There is no agreed-upon rule for deciding how much information of what kinds each citizen should have.

3. The loss of freedom involved in forcing people to acquire information would probably far outweigh the benefits to be gained from a better-informed electorate.

These obstacles compel most democratic governments to do little more than get their youths in schools to enroll in civics courses. This is one major reason democratic election systems always operate at less-than-perfect efficiency. Even more poignant is the fact that there is no more difficult task facing a modern democratic government than that of containing pressures toward excessive information, without at the same time encouraging practices of secrecy which choke off the flow of information upon which the vitality of government essentially depends.

Another paramount aspect of providers and availability of information is the wide variety of actions that can be taken to convey information. As Lewis Helm (1981:119) points out, the following questions are crucial in this regard:

1. How important is the announcement?
2. What audience will be affected most?
3. How complex is the issue?
4. In what context will the announcement be made? This would include other related concerns, the history of the subject, and plans for future releases.
5. What reaction is anticipated?
6. How does the announcement fit into the over-all public affairs plan?

In addition to these questions, media characteristics are important also and should be taken into consideration because, according to Helm (1981:119),

Television is the only source of news for almost two-thirds of all people (at least in the United States)--but it is not suitable for the explanation of complex issues and cannot focus on a well-defined audience.

Radio is a "hot" medium that can generate emotional support. However, it suffers a malady similar to television in that it cannot deal with complexity.

Newspapers can deal with story details in slightly more depth than broadcast. It is a medium where information can be seen in print and reproduced or clarified.

Magazines lack the timeliness of other media, but they can treat material in depth. They can also be selected to reach well-defined readers and can be reproduced in quantity for secondary distribution to target groups.

Since media characteristics can influence information content, media selection should be considered with the message as a package, instead of separately. The following instruments are suggested by Helm (1981:120-127) as means to orchestrate information to target audiences. Each of these instruments is discussed separately.

1. News or Press Release

This media instrument is the most basic and overused tool of information providers. It can set forth the specific facts of an invent, permitting the provider to go on record with an issue the way s/he wants the issue to be presented. It can be given out at news conferences. It can generate follow-up interest and be used to answer subsequent questions. The news release is print-oriented in that it does not emphasize the photo and broadcast potential.

2. Press Conference

The press conference facilitates the broad dissemination of announcements, provides a detailed explanation of complex issues, focuses on events and personal identification of an information provider with the issue, and encourages participation by all media. On the negative side, the press conference permits the presiding information provider to "misspeak" either intentionally or unintentionally, requires extensive preparation for participants, emphasizes foibles in the speaker's delivery, requires major public affairs support to manage, and permits little control over the message once it is released. Furthermore, if used too frequently, the press conference's attraction for reporters diminishes especially in the absence of a major running story to discuss.

3. Press Briefing

This is a less formal means of doing the same thing the press conference does. The press briefing is normally limited to a handful of reporters. Its ground rules can include everything "on the record" (fully usable), as "background" (without attribution by name), "deep background" (written as the reporter's own thoughts), and "off the record" (the discussion never took place). Only selected media are usually invited and ground rules allow the information provider to answer questions without public attribution. For this reason, an increasing number of reporters no longer participate in any but "on the record" sessions. Another problem is that nothing said, even though it is termed "off the record," can be guaranteed as secret.

4. Press Availability

Press availability refers to the fact that the information provider will be present and respond to a broad range of questions and pose for photos or television. It is normally used when an event occurs. However, to the degree that press availability might become too low key to attract a large audience, except in the case of a head of state or other very top personality, it adds informality to the occasion.

5. Radio Actuality

This is the radio equivalence of the news release. Information providers tape the voice of an official, then telephone it to radio stations. Other information providers connect the tape with a "call-in" telephone number so that stations can make their own tapes of an announcement as though they attended the news conference.

6. Television Actuality

Like radio actuality, television actuality is the television equivalence of the news release. Television actuality refers to a TV news clip produced by information providers and mailed to interested television stations. Since television clips cannot be timely for breaking news, they generally provide feature material. Smaller television stations have become the major consumers of TV clips because these stations lack the capability to develop material independently. A negative aspect of television actuality is that a policy-maker might accuse providers of TV clips of "propaganda" if s/he disagrees with the issue being publicized. Another negative aspect of this instrument is its high cost.

7. Op-Ed Pieces

These refer to major "thought" pieces written by opinion leaders about some aspect of policy or the manner in which a program is being implemented. These pieces are normally about 500-700 words long and were so named because they appear on the page opposite the editorial page. Op-ed pieces are highly controlled forms of communications and are capable of expressing in exact and detailed manner the intent of the information provider. However, since op-ed pieces rarely can be developed on a timely basis, and because the number of publications using them, while growing, is very limited, these instruments have a limited audience.

8. Features

Publications and broadcast media always seek feature material. Thus, information providers' research into a different "angle" could potentially interest media reaching a variety of audiences. One difficulty with features is that considerable effort must be invested on speculation without commitment of interest from the media. Another difficulty is that the material is liable to be rewritten once released. There is also the potential for information providers to be charged with attempting to "promote" a policy or a service through propaganda.

9. Conferences and Seminars

In order to develop in-depth understanding among the media and related groups, conferences and seminars are used. The difficulties involved in using these instruments include (a) the amount of effort required to plan and conduct the meetings and (b) the inability to control what is said and how it is reported.

10. Magazine Articles

These are similar to op-ed pieces in many ways. However, magazine articles can more directly focus on interested groups. To prepare magazine articles, considerable work is needed and such work always must be done on speculation. Furthermore, unless the article is an integral part of a long-term public affairs plan, timeliness is rare.

11. Special Interviews

Since many media representatives normally request personal interviews with policy-makers, selection can be made by issue, by region, and by interest group. Preparation for an interview can range from minor to very major, depending on the familiarity of the official to be interviewed. What is most important is knowledge of the interviewing medium. Some reporters, especially those working on television specials with predetermined story lines, frequently will interview an official for upwards of an hour, then use only a small segment that fits their story line. Seeing this strategy as the worst form of special interviews, many government officials now refuse to participate in TV specials unless they retain some control over the segment that is finally used. When this demand is made, the reporter involved generally reports that the official refused to be interviewed, misrepresenting the circumstances while adding to the thrust of the story. Some government officials have learned how to voice their big thoughts in terse (30 seconds or less) non-editable terms.

12. Congressional (Legislative) Testimony

While this instrument should provide one of the best opportunities to communicate a point of view to the legislators and to interested publics, it is usually the worst in actual practice. Protocol demands that legislators see the testimony before the media. If legislators disagree with it, they may leak selected parts of a testimony in advance of the information provider's appearance and refute those parts publicly before the hearing is held. As a consequence, the actual testimony can become a non-event. With many hearings being held at the same time, only those involving major national or international issues get media coverage. In addition, only a small portion of a full testimony normally is read by the witness and the rest is inserted into the record.

Faced with a deadline, a reporter does not have the opportunity to hear a testimony on complex issues before s/he writes a story. As such, coverage of committee hearings often comprises of reaction statements about stands which have never been reported initially. In essence, the whole system of testifying works against a sound communication between various branches of government.

13. Brochures

Brochures are excellent means for reproducing definitive articles about issues and conveying information to target groups without the use of mass media. These instruments range from inexpensive to high quality slick pieces. Like the pile of news clips, brochures are also another means of showing "action" by their providers.

14. Periodicals

Periodicals are published by government agencies to disseminate important information to citizens. They are especially critical for maintaining contact with groups that have a continuing interest in programs and policies. Periodicals can also be used to promote programs in an effort to generate increased funding for an agency. As target groups multiply and the ability to reach them becomes more difficult, an agency tends to proliferate its production of periodicals.

15. Displays

These instruments are very effective for communicating a "point of sale" message. The problem with displays is that their cost per contact tends to be far higher than communications through mass media. Thus, use of displays are usually limited to very specific purposes. While in African, Asian, Australian, Caribbean, European, and Latin American countries the use of displays is emphasized, only minor use is made of them in the United States.

16. Speeches

Speeches usually serve as the basic activity around which other public affairs activities are built. For example, if a speech is to be made about social services by a policy-maker to a target group, it can be mechanized through other available outlets: editors and reporters, television shows, dinner sessions, etc. Put differently, while the social services speech would reach only the targeted group, proper orchestration of the secondary audiences should bring high returns.

17. Slide Presentations

These instruments can be used effectively to support explanations of complex issues. However, except the presentation is professionally handled and the slides add interest, rather than compete with the speaker for interest, there is a risk of losing the audience when the lights go out.

18. Films

Films are used to describe government agencies, to promote issues, to train personnel, to be placed on television, etc. Like brochures and news-clips, films can show that an agency has been active without necessarily demonstrating that a target audience has been reached.

19. Congressional (Legislative) Record

This is an instrument that is uniquely available in government to reach the audience, and one that brings great prestige with it. A legislative member can write a laudatory statement about an agency that has done an outstanding job in an area of interest in the Record. On certain occasions, a member will insert statements written by the agency.

20. Government Printing Offices

Government printing offices serve as focal points for the purchase, printing, and binding of all publications developed by governments. These offices produce almost everything from telephone answering pads to slick color magazines. Government printing offices operate under rigid costs and quality criteria.

21. Leaks

As defined earlier, "leaks" are planted stories used to either support or oppose a public policy. A typology of leaks, which is based on who does the leaking and why, includes the following: (a) Candid Leak--a self-serving story that claims to convey the "truth," separating the information provider from the agency; (b) Leaks that Float--the release of information to obtain reactions which are used to make policy decisions; (c) Leaks from Torpedoes--when stories are directed toward nullifying a planned agency action; (d) Leaks and Swamps--overt means of getting stories out by acting as a concerned citizen.

The preceding instruments are used to orchestrate the flow of information to the various publics in democratic societies. The use of each instrument is dictated often by an information provider's degree of understanding, audience selectivity, and message content.

Finally, another major aspect of providers and availability of information has to do with the organizing and communicating effort which calls for many different decisions to be made. As Ray Hiebert (1981:8) suggests, in order for one to organize and communicate, s/he must first decide upon one or more of the following four different strategies:

1. Withholding
2. Releasing
3. Staging
4. Persuading

According to Hiebert (1981:8-13), in each of these strategies, a variety of techniques can be employed, each to a different effect. The process of organizing and communicating the effort is presented in Figure 3, which is followed by a discussion of each component.

Figure 3:
A Model of Government Communication
(A modified version of Hiebert's Model 1981:9)

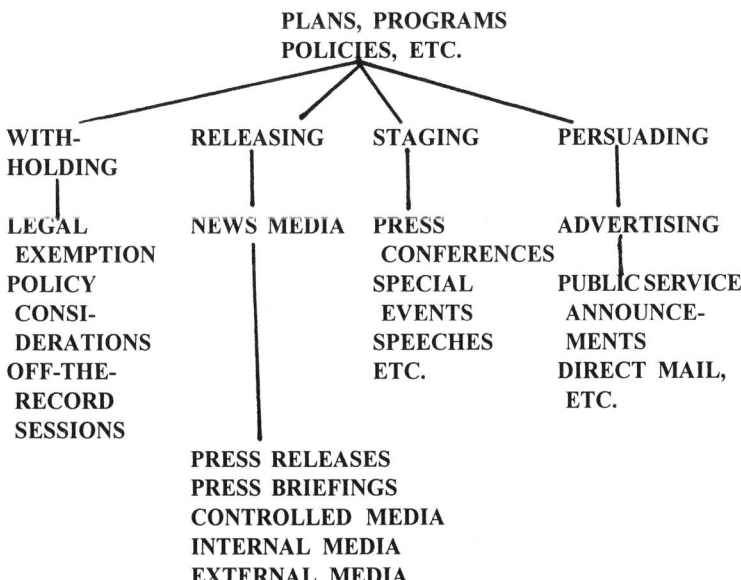

1. Withholding

Often a legitimate strategy, withholding information can be based on both legal and strategic reasons. We personally exercise this strategy everyday: we wear clothes to cover up those parts of our bodies we do not want others to see; we conceal some details about our past; we underplay some of our defects and mistakes. As the saying goes, "we put our best foot forward."

In order to lead, government officials must also protect themselves. However, those officials who hide fraud and corruption run serious risks of such actions backfiring and losing their credibility. In democratic societies, secrecy is an anathema; citizens dislike secret police, secret societies, and secret governments. People become quite suspicious about decisions that are not arrived at openly. Thus, withholding information as a strategy carries great risks and is usually not the most prudent way to communicate. Nonetheless, there are times when those risks are to be taken. The following are three ways information can be withheld:

(a) *Legal Exemptions* make it possible for governments to legally withhold information to protect national security, to protect individual privacy, and to protect certain business interests. Therefore, while governments in democratic societies cannot censor the press, they can at least censor themselves.

(b) *Policy Considerations* call for common sense, practical wisdom, and experienced judgment to determine what information should or should not be released to the public and *when* it should be released. Policy considerations are important in diplomatic negotiations, information that might affect the stock market, and in a number of other areas that concern the public.

(c) *Off-the-Record Sessions* provide governments some options in dealing with information and difficult circumstances. This strategy allows information providers to withhold information by giving it to reporters on the condition that they do not use it. The major purpose of these sessions is to provide reporters with background materials and explanations, making it possible for them to do a better job of interpreting a situation.

2. Releasing

Releasing information is a relatively more effective communication strategy than withholding information. When the information provider takes the initiative to get information out, s/he gains an advantage over his/her competitors. Social scientists have long demonstrated with empirical evidence that human beings are far more likely to believe the initial version of a story they hear than subsequent versions. However, the way in which information is released has a great effect on the message that is received. Thus, it behooves the information provider to consider carefully the method s/he chooses to release information. The first decision s/he must make is whether to release information to and through the news media, or through the government's own media: press releases, press briefings, controlled media, internal media, and external media. Let us look at each of these media, some of which have been discussed earlier in a different context.

(a) *The News Media* are neither owned nor controlled by the government in a modern democratic society. They are privately owned, and their owners are astutely independent and go to lengths to protect their rights and freedom. They perceive themselves as representatives of their listeners, readers, and viewers; they envision themselves as ombudsmen for the people and as watchdogs keeping an eye on government. Even though the government loses control of a message when the government releases it to the media, it nevertheless gains much needed circulation and credibility.

(b) *Press Releases*, as stated earlier, have been the traditional method of getting government information to the news media. In the right circumstances for the appropriate situation, press releases can be quite useful.

(c) *Press Briefings*, as noted previously, are probably more useful than press releases. Press briefings permit reporters more control over a message and allow them to ask questions and influence information flow.

(d) *Controlled Media* refer to publications or productions owned by the government. Their production is growing rapidly.

(e) *Internal Media* include employee newsletters, magazines, etc. They are essential to organizational communication in government, in education, in industry, and in all other areas where people work together in groups. While internal media have limited impact on the mass public, they are nonetheless very important to their target publics.

(f) *External Media* are used to supplement the information released to the news media, but the former could never replace the latter. Governments use published books and magazines to fill an information void left by the news media.

3. Staging

In an age when so many different interest groups are competing for a limited amount of time and space in the media, staging events is perhaps the best way of getting a message into the news media. However, staging can be a very difficult activity. Simply stated, staging calls for arranging a situation in such a way that it attracts the attention of the news media and gets news coverage. Much of what occurs in government and politics in contemporary democratic societies involves the jockeying of political factions or interest groups for public attention by staging events. Thus, staging requires skill, intelligence, imagination, thorough preparation, and good timing. Nonetheless, staging cannot be overused. The following are the media used for staging:

(a) *Press Conferences*, as stated earlier, are staged events through which policy-makers put themselves on the firing line to win news attention. These information providers must be carefully rehearsed and thoroughly prepared so that an event does not backfire.

(b) *Special Events* include anniversaries, open houses, conferences, caucuses, conventions, and other special situations exploited by policy-makers to get news coverage.

(c) *Speeches*, as noted previously, are commonly used in staging an event to get publicity. Even though the news media have learned not to be easily exploited by information providers, the principle still remains.

4. Persuading

Persuasion is a legitimate and necessary strategy governments in democratic societies employ. Since facts and information may not always be sufficient to lead the people, there are times when government officials have to persuade citizens to do what is required to run a country. It cannot be overemphasized that a politician in a democratic society must persuade the people to vote for him/her in the first place, so s/he can get elected to office and set up the government to keep the people informed. Media used for persuasion include the following:

(a) *Advertising* makes it possible for a government to state its case for its own purpose by buying its own time or space in the mass media.

(b) *Public Service Announcements* also make it possible for a government to package its own persuasive messages. A government in a democratic society can often get free advertising for announcement packages because of the requirement that radio and television must use some air time for public service.

(c) *Direct Mail* is used to get a specific message to a specific group with maximum accuracy and minimum cost. The combination of direct mail, demographic data, and the computer has brought about a revolution in targeting communication.

The preceding discussion about strategies and techniques, as they exist in theory and as they are practiced in all aspects of government in a democratic society, is an attempt to model the communication process, to see how it all fits together, how each part relates to the others, and how the whole can be placed into an understandable context. By treating communication as a process, it can be seen that it has many parts. Communication involves more than just sending out messages. The messages are affected by all the parts of the process, including the media by which they are carried, the publics that receive them, and the reactions and responses they evoke. Should any of the elements of the process be ignored, the results can be ruined.

Uses of Information

In a modern democratic society, information is principally used for (1) decision-making, (2) political participation, (3) education, (4) conflict resolution, (5) nation-building, and (6) international relations. Each of these six interrelated uses of information is discussed separately.

1. Decision-Making

The only information a rational voter, for example, is interested in is that which will allow him/her to change his/her preliminary voting decision, i.e. the decision indicated by his/her first estimate of his/her party differential[19]. Since information is costly, only the information that provides the voter returns in terms of a better decision or increased confidence in the present one is rational to acquire (Downs 1957:241).

---

[19] *Party differential* as used here refers to a set of characteristics (e.g., quality of leadership, membership, political ideology, etc.) that distinguishes one political party from other parties.

To find out whether a given bit of information might change a voter's mind, s/he will compare it with his/her estimated party differential. When one of the parties is elected, the information which the bit contains can then be translated into a positive, negative, or zero change in the utility income[20] the voter expects. Since the latter is the difference between the utility income s/he expects if the incumbents are reelected and the one s/he expects if the rivals win, the change will directly affect the voter's party differential. The voter will acquire the bit of information, if there is a reasonable chance that the party differential s/he now has will be completely negated by the change this bit indicates (Downs 1957:241).

However, it is not easy for a citizen to estimate what change his/her party differential s/he can expect from a given bit of information. The order in which they are acquired becomes crucial because bits are not independent of each other. Furthermore, it is difficult to convert a bit's expected value into its expected payoff. A voter can only know three things about each bit before s/he acquires it: (1) its cost, (2) its possible value, and (3) the probability associated with each value. Moreover, this knowledge is really a set of subjective estimates based on the available information already acquired (Downs 1957:241-242).

Thus, the following conclusions can be drawn it terms of the use of information in decision-making. First, for those voters who care about who wins, information is relatively useless. Second, for those voters who do not care about who wins, information is most useful. In essence, no rational voter has a very high incentive to acquire political information.

2. Political Participation

Information has the potential to enlarge participation in power, wealth, and prestige and to restrict it. Restricted political participation eventually means that one group is dominated by another. Concretely, not having certain information can prevent citizens from participating in the most important activities in their own political system; it can

---

[20]*Utility income* is the benefit or satisfaction expected from a particular choice or course of action.

reduce them to the passive objects of judicial and bureaucratic actions without control over their material condition.

3. Education

Diplomas and degrees are tickets permitting entrance to the professions, the best positions in business firms, and jobs in the civil service--a major employer in most countries. The information chosen as the medium for knowledge at all levels of education contributes to patterns of access to the most prestigious and intellectually superior diploma-granting academic institutions. For this reason, it is not surprising that the debate about which information to impart to students has grown sharper.

Resistance to changes in the information to be provided to students comes from many quarters, including that of teachers who fear for their jobs and anticipate a change in academic standards. It also comes from those who fear that their own high status, which depends in part on the possession of certain information, will be threatened. A different source of opposition is the argument that unless a society enjoys or promotes uniform information, it risks political division in the long run.

4. Conflict Resolution

Disagreements over what information to impart to citizens (which can be disagreements about who shall participate in power, wealth, and prestige) are a source of conflicts between ethnic groups, regions, and states. The conflicts that emerge are usually resolved by changing patterns in terms of what may be called nation-building.

5. Nation-Building

Choice of information contributes to the consolidation of communities called nations and the restructuring of these nations. As Karl Deutsch states, a nation is a "people who have learned to communicate with each other and to understand each other well beyond the mere interchange of goods and services" (Deutsch 1953:65). It is obvious that information is a basis of that communication and thus an instrument of consolidation. It is also one of the most powerful instruments for developing symbols of nationhood.

6. *International Relations*

How does information used in international business and in intergovernmental relations affect international relations? Certainly diplomatic information is a matter of choice, and is a form of capital possessed by some countries and elites but not others. In order to equalize access to information and to increase participation in world affairs, speakers of Esperanto, a created, non-national language, have proposed it for world organizations and diplomacy. However, even those who are obliged to learn diplomatic languages in special schools do not support such a proposal.

Examination of the preceding uses of information in modern democratic societies shows that such uses are neither passive nor inviolable. Information choices, linked with other political and economic choices, are made by leaders and elites to shape and direct societies.

Costs of Information

The types of costs[21] associated with obtaining information can be categorized as follows: (1) transmission costs, (2) differential costs, (3) communication costs, (4) delegated or shifting costs, and (5) opportunity costs. What follows is a discussion of each of these types of costs.

1. Transmission Costs

These are costs incurred from sending or transferring information from one person or place to another. For example, if a voter depends on an expert to evaluate the facts regarding new tax codes, there is a cost inherent in transmitting the expert's opinion to the voter. It is also likely that the expert him-/her-self may have had to pay for the gathering of data by others.

Downs divides transmission costs into two major classes as follows (1957:210):

> 1. *Transferable costs* can be shifted from the voter onto someone else. We separate transferable costs into three types: (a) *Procurement costs* are the costs of gathering, selecting, and transmitting data; (b) *Analysis costs* are the costs of making factual analysis of data; (c) *Evaluative costs* are the costs of relating data or factual analyses to specific goals; i.e. of evaluating them.

---

[21]*Costs* are subjective; they exist in the minds of decision-makers. They are based on expectations of how individuals would evaluate the alternatives given up. Costs can never be directly measured by someone other than the decision-makers because only they can place values on what are forgone. Costs, however, often have a monetary component that enables us to approximate their values. For example, the costs of attending a university are equal to the highest valued opportunities that are given up because of (a) the time necessary to attend and (b) the purchasing power (i.e. money) necessary to pay tuition and fees, buy books and supplies, etc. When there are good reasons to expect that monetary considerations are relatively unimportant, the monetary component will approximate the total costs of the options.

2. *Nontransferable costs* must be borne by the voter. Theoretically, every cost except that of going to the polls can be passed onto others.

Apparent from the preceding excerpt is the notion that any cost borne in transmitting information is a deflection of scarce resources from some utility-producing use. Put differently, the cost of transmitting information is a foregone alternative.

2. Differential Costs

These refer to costs relating to quantitative differences. In any society where an extensive division of labor and the presence of uncertainty exist, the cost of information will be different for different individuals. Hence, the amount of information it is rational for one individual to obtain may be much greater or much smaller than the amount it is rational for another individual to acquire. This proposition is valid, even when the returns from information are identical for everyone in a given society (Downs 1957:236).

Even if a society were populated by rational individuals with equal intelligence, equal interest in government policies, and equal incomes, they would still not be equally informed politically. Many of them might know practically nothing about politics because they delegated their decisions to others. The division of labor places individuals in different social locations with varying access to and needs for information, and lack of perfect knowledge prevents each individual from communicating his/her specialized knowledge to others without costs. Therefore, as Downs concludes (1957:236),

> 1. Any concept of democracy based on an electorate of equally well-informed citizens is irrational; i.e. it presupposes that citizens behave irrationally.
>
> 2. The foundations of differential political power in a democracy are rooted in the very nature of society.

In addition to these forces, the unequal distribution of income is another differentiating force. Since all information is costly, those with high incomes are in a relatively better position to obtain it than those with low incomes (Downs 1957:236). The cost of information being harder for low-income citizens to bear, more of them are likely to be uncertain because they lack information. And since uncertainty reduces the returns from voting, a lower proportion of low-income groups would vote, even if voting costs were equally difficult for everyone to bear (Downs 1957:273).

In the United States, for example, the effort to lessen differential information costs by using television as the major arbiter of information disparity has added significantly to the total cost of elections. As Dye and his partners reveal, "In 1986 alone $1.8 billion was spent on major elections, two-thirds of it on television. Between the 1984 and 1988 elections, $6 billion was raised and spent" (Dye et al 1993:196). It is obvious that there is a necessity of bearing economic costs in order to reduce the biases against citizens with low incomes in acquiring information.

3. Communication Costs

Significant differences exist between obtaining information in order to vote and obtaining it in order to influence policy-making. To begin with, voters automatically communicate their decision to government in the act of voting (see chapter three for details on this act), but policy influencers must transmit their opinions to government by specific act in order to achieve results. Like all acts, that of communication uses scarce resources and thus is costly. The amount of communication costs are determined by the citizen's position in society. If s/he is the Vice-President or the Deputy Prime Minister of a country, the costs will be low; if s/he is a minimum-wage employee in a rural area, the costs may be very high (Downs 1957:252).

Whatever communication costs turn out to be, someone must pay them. However, the person communicating need not be the one to pay them. If his/her interest in a policy area stems from his business, s/he can transfer the costs of transmitting his/her views to his firm, which will probably deduct them from its taxable income. Thus, the government and the firm bear the costs and the citizen is spared. But no matter who pays, whatever part of the costs fall on the policy influencer must be counted as part of the marginal costs to be balanced against whatever marginal returns there are from being informed. Since it is more expensive to reach some officials than to reach others, communication costs vary depending upon to whom in the government a citizen communicates his/her views. The opinion impact also depends upon whom the influencer is able to contact. Both these factors must be taken into account when deciding how much information to purchase for purposes of influencing policy (Downs 1957:252).

4. Delegated or Shifting Costs

Delegated or shifting costs are those costs some citizens assign to others. When a society becomes highly specialized, many areas of decision pose literally incomprehensible problems for those who lack expertise in them. Nonetheless, nonexperts often must have opinions concerning the appropriateness of policies in these areas so that they too can make important political choices. For example, the nature of public health in a contemporary society is a major issue both for the survival of the nation and for proper allocation of resources. But, public health issues are so complex that almost everyone who lacks expertise in the area has to rely for his/her opinions upon those who have the expertise.

As Downs (1957:231) observes, the division of labor creates this problem, but it also solves it in the sense that citizens can buy the generalized opinions of experts in each area at a much lower cost than they would incur by manufacturing comparable opinions of their own. He notes that the enormity of the saving would make rational political action in a large-sized democracy impossible, if the task of factual analysis is not shifted onto specialists. Downs also suggests that although shifting analysis of facts onto experts reduces the cost of such analysis, some costs must still be paid by the citizen. The only way the citizen can avoid paying such costs is to pass them on to subsidizers or gain access to the free information stream.

For a citizen to be a rational delegator, Downs (1957:232) proposes that s/he must personally determine whether the agent s/he selects (1) has goals that are similar to his/her own, (2) possesses more data than s/he does, and (3) has powers of judgment that are, at worst, not inferior to his/her own that they offset the advantages of better information. These conditions, according to Downs, are imperative in areas where the delegator plans to trust the agent's judgment. Thus, in order to trust a prospective agent, Downs suggests that a rational decision-maker must investigate the agent by checking the latter's past judgments. In essence, evaluative delegation often involves a cost of selecting agents.

5. Opportunity Costs

No discussion of information costs can be complete without examining the notion of opportunity costs: the highest valued benefits that must be sacrificed or foregone as the result of choosing an alternative (in this case, a particular bit of information). Scarcity calls the tune in acquiring information. We cannot have as much of every information as we would like. Information, like all things, is scarce or requires the use of scarce resources. How can we have more information and simultaneously accumulate more wealth? How can we increase our current consumption of information and simultaneously increase our savings accounts? The answer is, we cannot! The choice of one requires us to give up something of the other.

An unpleasant fact about information is that the choice to get more of some bits is, at the same time, a choice not to get other bits. The cost of any information is not the drudgery and undesirable aspects that may be associated with obtaining the information. The distinction between (a) the undesirable attributes of information and (b) the highest valued opportunity foregone in order to obtain the information is a fundamental distinction because only the latter can be considered a cost.

The preceding discussion about information costs clearly shows that information required for real-world decision-making is influenced by its costs. The likelihood that a particular bit of information will be acquired varies inversely with its cost to the decision-maker. So, it is implied in this book that differences (or changes) in information costs will influence how decisions are made.

Benefits of Information

That political information can be very useful or profitable to a citizen because it helps him/her make the best possible decisions is hardly a matter of dispute. While there are many benefits[22] that motivate citizens to acquire political information, two of them are paramount: (1) formulating their voting decisions, and (2) forming opinions with which they can influence government policy. A discussion of these two main benefits follows.

1. Voting

For the purposes of voting, a citizen's basic return on information is his/her party differential. It allows him/her to calculate the expected payoffs of various sets of information bits. The returns must be drastically reduced to match the infinitesimal role which each citizen's vote plays in deciding the election before being compared with the cost of data. Consequently, the returns are so minimal that many rational voters refrain from purchasing any political information *per se.* Instead, they rely upon free data obtained accidentally (Downs 1957:258).

2. Influencing Government Policy

In terms of influencing government policy-making in any area of decision, a citizen must be continuously well-informed about events in that area. S/he has to do more than the voter who merely deals with *post facto* differentials. The expense of such awareness is so exorbitant that no citizen can afford to absorb it in every policy area, even if by doing so s/he could discover places where his/her intervention would yield large profits. If s/he is to exercise any influence at all, s/he must limit his/her awareness to areas where

---

[22]Some citizens find excitement in arguing about politics or following campaigns; others gain social prestige at cocktail parties by demonstrating their knowledge about current affairs. No matter how political the content of such information, it is obtained for the purpose of entertainment.

intervention pays off most and information costs least. These are the areas of his/her production specialization because his/her income flows from them and s/he is already well-informed about them (Downs 1957:258-259).

In sum, voting and influencing government policy in democratic societies are great benefits that can be derived from acquiring political information. Voting itself is a device for influencing future government policies by selecting representatives who have made specific promises. Voting has also already influenced past policies in the sense that the government's actions were conditioned by how it thought citizens would vote. Thus, as far as the government is concerned, there is very little difference between the uses of information to vote or to influence government policy.

Conclusion

What we have attempted to demonstrate in this chapter is the important role ***information state*** plays in shaping political behavior. The tenor of the discussion is that in order for us to understand political life in a democratic society, it behooves us to understand the impact of information.

When citizens engage in conflict, they derive the meanings of the conflict from information. Information not only provides meanings for abstract ideas and ideologies, it also defines political institutions and provides our images of political leaders and voters. What citizens think, feel, and do in politics arise out of the meanings they attach to events, the perceptions they have of government institutions, and the attitudes they have toward personalities. These events, institutions, and personalities are presented to them through the information media: books, magazines, movies, newspapers, press releases, public speeches, radio, television, and so on.

Meanings, perceptions, and attitudes do not emerge in advance of events and personalities, but in the process of disseminating and acquiring information. Information is not a mere transmission link; information itself creates meanings, perceptions, and attitudes. It is true, of course, that citizens frequently screen out, or reinterpret, information that differs from their preconceived notions. But these preconceived notions were formed with the help of numerous previous information. Simply stated, information is not neutral.

Political information is very important in a democratic society. What leaders *say* is just as important as what they *do*. First of all, political information provides reassurance to citizens that government leaders care about them. Even if government policies do not succeed in eliminating most of society's problems, it is still imperative that government *says* it wants to solve these problems. The statements of a government may inform citizens more about the aspirations of that society and its leadership than about actual conditions.

Second, political information provides means of *participation* in civic life. Citizens can *participate* in politics by passively watching their television sets or listening to their radios, responding with pride, patriotism, anger, or cynicism as the drama of politics unfolds (a thorough treatment of this aspect appears in chapter five).

Finally, political information provides *legitimacy* to both the government and public policies in the sense that citizens can come to accept as law the actions of government. Democratic institutions--i.e. campaigns, elections, political parties, etc.--lend additional legitimacy to government acts. Citizens are instructed that they must obey the law because they had an opportunity, however indirect, to participate in the making of the law. Thus, citizens of a democratic society have a greater obligation to obey the law than citizens living under dictatorial rule. Nonetheless, *all* modern societies--dictatorial or democratic, capitalist or socialist--use information channels to *legitimize* the authority of their governments.

Bibliography

Akagha, Fidelis S. E. (1985). *Strategies for Economic Development in Africa.* New York: Vantage Books.

Alford, Robert R. (1963). *Party and Society.* Chicago: Rand McNally.

Amin, Samir (1976). *Unequal Development.* New York: Monthly Review Press.

Anderson, Charles W.; Mehden, Fred R. von der; and Young, Crawford (1967). *Issues of Political Development.* Englewood Cliffs, New Jersey: Prentice-Hall, Incorporated.

Anderson, James E. (1982). *Cases in Public Policy-Making.* New York: Holt, Rinehart and Winston.

Andrain, Charles F. (1983). *Foundations of Comparative Politics: A Policy Perspective.* Monterey, California: Brooks/Cole Publishing Company.

Angeles, P. A. (1981). *Dictionary of Philosophy.* New York: Barnes and Noble Books.

Angelopoulos, Angelos (1976). *For a New Policy of International Development.* New York: Praeger Publishers.

Arnold, R. Douglas (1990). *The Logic of Congressional Action.* New Haven: Yale University Press.

Bangura, Abdul Karim (1994). 'Semantic Representation With and Without Logic.' *Languages of Design* (Vol. 2).

Bartel, M. Larry (1991). 'Constituency Opinion and Congressional Policy Making: The Reagan Defense Buildup.' *American Political Science Review* (Vol. 85).

Beauchamp, Tom L. and Pinkard, Terry P. eds. (1983). *Ethics and Public Policy*. Englewood Cliffs: Prentice-Hall, Incorporated.

Becker, Gary (1983). *The Economic Approach to Human Behavior*. Chicago: University of Chicago Press.

Bell, Roderick A. and Edwards, David E. (1974). *American Government: The Facts Reorganized*. Morristown, New Jersey: General Learning Press.

Berelson, R. Bernard; Lazarsfeld, Paul; and Mcphee, William (1954). *Voting: A Study of Opinion Formation in a Presidential Election*. Chicago: University of Chicago Press.

Bobiash, Donald (1992). *South-South Aid*. New York: Saint Martin's Press.

Boesak, Allan (1977). *A Socio-Ethical Study on Black Theology and Power*. New York: Orbis Books.

Boesak, Allan (1984). *Black and Reformed: Apartheid, Liberation, and the Calvinist Tradition*. New York: Orbis Books.

Bolling, Landrum R. (1982). *Private Foreign Aid*. Boulder, Colorado: Westview Press.

Brent, Stephen (1990). 'Aiding Africa.' *Foreign Policy* (Fall, No. 80).

Brewster, Lawrence G. (1984). *The Political Agenda*. New York: Saint Martin's Press.

Brigham, John and Brown, Don W. eds. (1980). *Policy Implementation*. Berkely: University of California Press.

Brown, Robert S. (1984). 'Conditionality: A New Form of Colonialism?' *Africa Report* (Vol. 29, No. 5).

Browne, Stephen (1990). *Foreign Aid in Practice*. New York: New York University Press.

Burnham, D. Walter (1982). *The Current Crisis in American Politics*. New York: Oxford University Press.

Burns, James Macgregor (1978). *Leadership*. New York: Harper and Row.

Caldiera, A. Gregor; Patterson, C. Samuel; and Markko, A. Gregory (1990). 'The Mobilization of Voters in Congressional Elections.' *Journal of Politics* (Vol. 47).

Campbell, Argus; Converse, Philip; Miller, Warren; and Stokes, Donald (1964). *The American Voter*. New York: John Wiley and Sons.
Cassen, Robert (1986). *Does Aid Work?* Oxford: Clarendon Press.
Chilcote, Ronald H. (1981). *Theories of Comparative Politics: The Search for a Paradigm*. Boulder, Colorado: Westview Press.
Clor, Harry M., ed. (1974). *The Mass Media and Modern Democracy*. Chicago: Rand McNally College Publishing Company.
Clough, Michael (1992). *U.S. Policy Toward Africa and the End of the Cold War*. New York: Council on Foreign Relations Press.
Conway, Margaret (1985). *Political Participation in The U.S.* Washington, DC: Congressional Quarterly Press.
Converse, Philip (1964). 'The Nature of Belief Systems in Mass Publics.' David Apter (ed). *Ideology and Discontent*. New York: Free Press.
Converse, Philip (1976). *The Dynamics of Party Support: Cohorts Analyzing Party Identification*. Beverly Hills, California: Sage Publications.
Copi, Irving M. (1979). *Symbolic Logic* (5th ed). New York: Macmillan Publishing Company, Incorporated.
Cord, Robert L.; Medeiros, James A.; Jones, Walter S.; and Roskin, Michael G. (1985). *Political Science* (2nd ed). Englewood Cliffs, New Jersey: Prentice-Hall, Incorporated.
Creedy, John ed. (1990). *Foundations of Economic Thought*. Oxford: Basil Blackwell Limited.
David, Wilfred L. (1985). *The IMF Policy Paradigm*. New York: Praeger Publishers.
David, Wilfred L. (1986). *Conflicting Paradigms in the Economics of Developing Nations*. New York: Praeger Publishers.
David, Wilfred L. (1988). *Political Economy of Economic Policy: The Quest for Human Betterment*. New York: Praeger Publishers.
Denham, John (1986). 'The Fleecing of the World's Poor.' *New Statesman* (April 18).
Denham, John and Beasle, Robert (1987). 'Debt--Who Pays?' *New Statesman* (July 17).

Deutsch, Karl W. (1953). *Nationalism and Social Communication: An Inquiry into the Foundations of Nationality* (2nd ed). Cambridge, Massachusetts: Massachusetts Institute of Technology.

Downs, Anthony (1957). *An Economic Theory of Democracy.* New York: Harper and Row Publishers, Incorporated.

Du Bois, W. E. B. (1981). *The World and Africa* (12th ed). United States of America: International Publishers Company, Incorporated.

Dumont, René (1983). *Stranglehold on Africa.* London: Andre Deutsch.

Duverger, Maurice (1954). *Political Party* (translated by Barbara North and Robert North). New York: John Wiley and Sons.

Dye, Thomas R.; Zeigler, Harmon; and Lichter, S. Robert (1992). *American Politics in the Media Age* (4th ed). Pacific Grove, California: Brooks/Cole Publishing Company.

Eldersweld, J. Samuel (1982). *Political Parties in American Society.* New York: Basic Books.

Epstein, Leone D. (1976). *Political Parties in Western Democracies.* New York: Praeger Publishers.

Fieldhouse, D. K. (1986). *Black Africa.* Boston: Unwin Hyman.

Fiorina, P. Morris (1977). *Congress: Keystone of the Washington Establishment.* New Haven: Yale University Press.

Gaventa, John (1980). *Power and Powerlessness.* Urbana, Chicago: University of Illinois Press.

Goulet, Denis (1974). *A New Moral Order: Studies in Development Ethics and Liberation Theology.* Maryknoll: Orbis Books.

Goulet, Denis (1977). *The Cruel Choice: A New Critique in the Theory of Development.* New York: Athenaeum.

Greenberg, Edward S. (1974). *Serving the Few.* New York: John Wiley and Sons, Incorporated.

Gwartney, James D.; Stroup, Richard; and Clark, J. R. (1985). *Essentials of Economics* (2nd ed). Orlando, Florida: Academic Press, Incorporated.

Hadenius, Stig (1985). *Swedish Politics During the 20th Century.* Stockholm: The Swedish Institute.

Haggard, Steven and Kaufman, Robert P. eds. (1992). *The Politics of Economic Adjustment.* New Jersey: Princeton University Press.

Halberstadt, W. H. (1974). *An Introduction to Modern Logic.* Dubuque, Iowa: Kendall/Hunt Publishing Company.

Hammar, Tomas (1977). *The First Immigrant Election.* Stockholm: Commission on Immigration Research.

Hance, William A. (1958). *African Economic Development.* New York: Harper and Brothers.

Helm, Lewis M. (1981). 'Strategic Use of the Newsmedia.' Lewis M. Helm, et al (eds). *Informing the People.* New York: Longman, Incorporated.

Herbst, Jeffrey (1992). *U.S. Economic Policy Toward Africa.* New York: Council on Foreign Relations Press.

Hiebert, Ray Eldon (1981). 'A Model of the Government Communication Process.' Lewis M. Helm, et al (eds). *Informing the People.* New York: Longman, Incorporated.

Hospers, John (1967). *Introduction to Philosophical Analysis.* Englewood Cliffs, New Jersey: Prentice-Hall, Incorporated.

Hospers, John (1983). *Human Conduct.* New York: Harcourt, Brace, and World.

Hurley, P. J. (1993). *A Concise Introduction to Logic.* Belmont, California: Wadsworth Publishing Company.

Iverson, Torben (1994). 'Political Leadership and Representation in Western European Democracies: A Test of Three Models of Voting.' *American Journal of Political Science* (Vol. 38, No. 1).

Jackman, Robert (1987). 'Political Institutions and Voter Turnout in the Industrialized Democracies.' *American Political Science Review* (Vol. 81, No. 2).

Jacobson, Gary C. and Kernell, Samuel (1983). *Strategy and Choice in Congressional Elections.* New Haven: Yale University Press.

Katznelson, I. and Kesselman, M. (1979). *The Politics of Power: A Critical Introduction to American Government.* New York: Harcourt Brace Jovanovich, Incorporated.

Ladd, Everett Carll (1982). *Where Have All the Voters Gone?* New York: W. W. Norton and Company.

Lazarsfeld, Paul; Berelson, R. Bernard; and Gaudet, Hazel (1944). *The People's Choice.* New York: Columbia University Press.

Leuthold, David E. (1968). *Electioneering in a Democracy.* New York: John Wiley and Sons, Incorporated.

Lindblom, Charles E. (1968). *The Policy-Making Process.* Englewood Cliffs, New Jersey: Prentice-Hall, Incorporated.

Mancur, Olson (1971). *The Logic of Collective Action.* Cambridge, Massachusetts: Harvard University Press.

Mannheim, Karl (1955). *Ideology and Utopia.* New York: Harcourt, Brace and Company (Harvest Book Series).

Mayhew, David R. (1974). *Congress: The Electoral Connection.* New Haven: Yale University Press.

McGinnis, Joe (1969). *The Selling of the President 1968.* New York: Simon and Schuster.

McKenna, G. and Feingold, S. (1991). *Taking Sides: Clashing Views on Controversial Political Issues.* Guilford, Connecticut: The Duskin Publishing Group, Incorporated.

Miller, Arthur H. (1981). 'Policy Directions and Presidential Leadership: Alternative Interpretations of the 1980 Presidential Election' (paper presented at the American Political Science Association annual meeting).

Miller, Warren and Levitin, Teresa (1976). *Leadership and Change: The New Politics and the American Electorate.* Cambridge, Massachusetts: Winthrop.

Mitchell, William C. (1971). *Why Vote.* Chicago: Markham Publishing Company.

Mitchell, William C. (1974). 'Voting Dilemmas and the Logic of Choice.' Warner Feld, Alan T. Leonhard, and Walter W. Toxey, Jr. (eds). *The Enduring Questions of Politics.* Englewood Cliffs, New Jersey: Prentice-Hall, Incorporated.

Nanda, Ved P.; Shepherd, George W,; and McCarthy-Arnolds, Eileen (1993). *World Debt and the Human Condition: Structural Adjustment and the Right to Development.* New York: Greenwood Press.

Nelson, R. J. (1989). *The Logic of the Mind.* Norwell, Massachusetts: Kluwer Academic Press.

Nie, Norman; Verba, Sydney; and Petrocik, John (1976). *The Unchanging American Voter.* Cambridge, Massachusetts: Harvard University Press.

Niemi, Richard G. and Weissberg, Herbert F. eds. (1976). *Controversies in American Voting Behavior.* San Francisco, California: W. H. Freeman and Company.

Oruka, Henry Odera (1989). 'The Philosophy of Foreign Aid: A Question of the Right to a Human Minimum.' *Praxis International* (Vol. 8, No. 4).

Palfrey, R. Thomas and Rosenthal, Howard (1985). 'Voter Participation and Strategic Uncertainty.' *American Political Science Review* (Vol. 79).

Palfrey, R. Thomas and Lockerbie, Brad (1993). 'Party Contracting and Political Participation.' *American Journal of Political Science* (Vol. 38, No. 1).

Parenti, Michael (1974). *Democracy for the Few*. New York: Saint Martin's Press.

Parsons, Talcott (1937/1949). *The Structure of Social Action*. New York: McGraw-Hill (1937 ed); Glencoe, Illinois: The Free Press (1949 ed).

Parsons, Talcott (1951). *The Social System*. Glencoe, Illinois: The Free Press.

Patterson, Thomas E. and McClure, Robert D. (1976). *The Unseeing Eye: The Myth of Television Power in National Elections*. New York: G. P. Putnam's Sons.

Pomper, Gerald (1975). *Voters' Choice: Varieties of American Electoral Behavior*. New York: Dodd, Mead.

Rake, Alan (1988). 'Breaking the Debt Cycle.' *New African* (Vol. 249, June).

Rawls, John (1971). *A Theory of Justice*. Cambridge: Harvard University Press.

Reinard, John C. (1991). *Foundations of Argumentation: Effective Communication for Critical Thinking*. Dubuque, Iowa: The William C. Brown Publishers.

Riddel, J. Barry (1992). 'Things Fall Apart Again: Structural Adjustment Programs in Sub-Saharan Africa.' *Journal of Modern African Studies* (Vol. 30, No. 1).

Rodney, Walter (1982). *How Europe Underdeveloped Africa*. Washington, DC: Howard University Press.

Rousseau, Jean-Jacques (1950). *The Social Contract*. New York: Dutton Press.

Runes, D. D. ed. (1955). *Treasury of Philosophy*. New York: The Philosophical Library.

Sandbrook, Richard (1993). *The Politics of Africa's Economic Recovery*. Cambridge: Cambridge University Press.

Schattschneider, E. E. (1942). *Party Government*. New York: Ringhart Publication.

Schattschneider, E. E. (1960/1975). *The Semisovereign People: A Realist View of Democracy in America.* New York: Holt, Rinehart and Winston (1960 ed); Hinsdale, Illinois: The Dryden Press (1975 ed).

Schumpeter, Joseph A. (1943/1950). *Capitalism, Socialism and Democracy.* London: Allen and Unwin.

Seligson, Mitchell A. (1984). *The Gap Between Rich and Poor.* Boulder, Colorado: Westview Press.

Sender, John and Smith, Sheila (1986). *The Development of Capitalism in Africa.* New York: Methuen.

Shepherd, George W. (1987). 'Global Majority Rights: The African Context.' *Africa Today* (Vol. 34).

Shepherd, George W. (1990). 'The African Right to Development: World Policy and the Debt Crisis.' *Africa Today* (Vol. 37).

Shepherd, George W. and Anikpo, Mark O. C. eds. (1990). *Emerging Human Rights.* New York: Greenwood Press.

Sonko, Karamo N. M. (1990). 'Debt in the Eye of a Storm: The African Crisis in a Global Context.' *Africa Today* (Vol. 37, No. 4).

Sorauf, J. Frank (1967). 'Political Parties and Political Analysis.' William N. Chambers and Walter D. Burnham (eds). *The American Party System: Stages to Political Development.* New York: Oxford University Press.

Sorauf, J. Frank (1982). *Party Politics in America.* Boston: Little and Brown.

Stace, W. T. (1955). *The Philosophy of Hegel.* London: Dover Publications, Incorporated.

Stewart, Frances (1989). 'Basic Needs Strategies, Human Rights, and the Right to Development.' *Human Rights Quarterly* (Vol. 11).

Thiroux, Jacques P. (1990). *Ethics: Theory and Practice.* New York: Macmillan Publishing Company, Incorporated.

Times Mirror Center (1994). *The People, The Press and Politics: The New Political Landscape.* Los Angeles: The Times Mirror Center.

Tinder, Glen (1991). *Political Thinking: The Perennial Question.* New York: HarperCollins.

Titus, H. H. (1970). *Living Issues in Philosophy.* New York: Van Nostrand Reinhold Company.

Vallely, Paul (1990). 'Ethical Responsibility and Third World Debt.' *Cross Currents* (Vol. 41, No. 1).

Verba, Sydney; Schlozman, Kay Lehman; Brady, Harry; and Nie, Norman (1993). 'Citizen Activity: Who Participate? What do they say.' *American Political Science Review* (Vol. 87, No. 2).

Washington Post, The (1994). 'You Think Congress Is Out-Of-Touch: Look in the Mirror, Voters; The Trouble Starts With You' (Sunday 16:C1, C4).

Watson, Richard A. (1984). *The Presidential Contest*. New York: John Wiley and Sons.

Weber, Max (1947). *The Theory of Social and Economic Organization* (translated by A. M. Anderson and Talcott Parsons). New York: Oxford University Press.

Weissberg, Robert (1978). 'Collective Representation in Congress.' *American Political Science Review* (Vol. 72, No. 2).

Wielhouser, Peter and Lockerbie, Brad (1993). 'Party Contacting and Political Participation: 1952-1990.' *American Journal of Political Science* (Vol. 38, No. 1).

Winter, Herbert R. and Bellows, Thomas J. (1985). *People and Politics* (3rd ed). New York: John Wiley and Sons.

World Bank, The, (1993). *The World Bank Annual Report, 1993*. Washington, DC: World Bank Publications.

Indices

Name Index

A
Akagha, Fidelis, 25
Alford, Robert, 33
Anderson, Charles, 44
Andrain, Charles, 44-47
Angeles, P. A., 80
Arnold, R. Douglass, 92-93

B
Bangura, Abdul Karim, 81
Bartel, Larry, 97
Becker, Gary, 12-14, 17
Bell, Roderick, 40
Bellows, Thomas, 36 38-41, 43, 45

Berelson R. Bernard, 33, 101
Bertalanffy, Ludwig von, 78
Brandt, Willy, 35
Bryan, William Jennings, 34
Burke, Edmund, 42-43
Burnham, D. Walter, 103
Burns, James Macgregor, 100

C
Caldeira, A. Gregor, 106
Campbell, Angus, 33-34
Clark, J. R., 9
Clinton, Bill, 55, 58-59, 65, 86
Converse, Philip, 33-34
Conway, Margaret, 94
Copi, Irving M., 52, 56

Cord, Robert, 33-35, 37-38, 42-44
Creedy, John, 14

D
de Gaule, Charles, 35
Deutsch, Karl, 134-135
Downs, Anthony, 39, 109-118, 132-133, 136-142
Du Bois, W. E. B., 24
Duverger, Maurice, 48
Dye, Thomas, 110, 138

E
Easton, David, 16-17
Edwards, David, 40
Eldersweld, J. Samuel, 103
Elizabeth II, Queen, 42
Engels, Frederic, 82
Epstein, Leon, 34

F
Fieldhouse, D. K., 20
Fiorina, Morris P., 96

G
Gandhi, Mohandas, 70
Gaudet, Hazel, 33
Gaventa, John, 96
Gwartney, James, 9-10

H
Hadenius, Stig, 46
Halberstadt, W. H., 67
Hammar, Tomas, 37
Hegel, W. G., 80

Helm, Lewis, 119-120
Hiebert, Ray, 127
Hewitt, Don, 110
Hobbes, Thomas, 41
Hospers, John, 68, 70
Hurley, P. J., 65-66

I
Iverson, Torben, 95

J
Jackman, Robert, 106
Jackson, The Rev. Jesse, 36

K
Katznelson, I., 82-84
Kennedy, John F., 35, 70
Kesselman, M., 82-84
King, Jr., Martin Luther, 7, 65

L
Lazarsfeld, Paul, 33
Levitin, Teresa, 35
Lichter, Robert, 110
Lindblom, Charles E., 85
Locke, John, 41
Louis XIV of France, 45

M
Madison, James, 106
Mandela, Nelson, 71
Mannheim, Karl, 113
Marx, Karl, 82
McPhee, William, 33
Mehden, Fred, 44
Miller, Arthur, 35
Miller, Warren, 35

Mitchell, William, 32

N
Nelson, R., 52
Newell, Sara E., 74, 76
Nie, Norman, 34

O
Oruka, Henry Odera, 14-16, 18

P
Palfrey, R. Thomas, 105
Parenti, Michael, 84-85, 87
Parsons, Talcott, 30-31
Petrocik, John, 34
Pomper, Gerald, 34

R
Reagan, Ronald, 35
Reinard, John C., 71, 73-74, 76-78
Rockefeller, Jay, 101
Rodney, Walter, 22-24
Rosenthal, Howard, 105
Rousseau, Jean-Jacques, 41, 91
Runes, D. D., 69, 87

S
Sandbrook, Richard, 16-17, 19, 25-26
Schattschneider, E. E., 32, 38-39, 83, 87, 103

Schumpeter, Joseph A., x, 94-95
Shepherd, George, 25
Sorauf, J. Frank, 104-105
Stace, W. T., 80-81
Stroup, Richard, 9

T
Thiroux, Jacques P., 53-54
Tinder, Glen, 91
Titus, H. H., 81
Trudeau, Pierre Elliot, 35

V
Verba, Sydney, 34, 92-93

W
Watson, Richard, 33-35
Weber, Max, 30
Weissberg, Robert, 97-99
Wielhouser, Peter, 105
Winfrey, Oprah, 110
Winter, Herbert, 36, 38-41, 43, 45

Y
Young, Crawford, 44

Z
Zeigler, Harmon, 110

Subject Index

A
ABC (20/20 television show), 110
ABC poll, 102
Absolute monarchs, 45
Accidental data, 116
Accommodationist group, 83
Accountability, types, 20
Action Structure, defined, 3, 29
Action types, defined, 30
Actual contextual influences, x
A-form proposition, 56-57
Africa(n), 16, 22-24, 26-27, 45, 125
African-American(s), 36-37, 43, 69
Age (variable), 37
Alaska, 8, 38
Albania, 36
Alternation, 61
American Association of Retired Persons (AARP), 106-107
American Medical Association (AMA), 107
American politics, defined, ix
Antithesis, 81
Area of residence (variable), 38
Arguments (basic types), 52-53
Asia(n), 24, 125
Athenian city-state, 47
Australia(n), 33, 125

B
Baghdad (Iraq), 66
Balanced ticket, 44
Basic human minimum, 15, 18, 21
Basic human needs, 14-15, 17
Behavioral Revolution, defined, 92
Bit (information), defined, 112
Brazil, 110
Bristol, 24
British Empire, 42
British Parliament, 42

C
Canada, 33, 35
Candidates' influence (variable), 35
Capitalist system, 22
Caribbean, 125
CBS (60 Minutes television show), 110
Chicanos, 37
China, Peoples Republic, 40, 46
Cocoa, 19
Cohesive Relations, 3, 51, 81, 88
Cold War, 27
Colonial rule, 45

Communist countries (former), 36
Comparative politics, defined, ix
Conclusion, defined, 52-53
Context, defined, x, 1
Context-renewing, 1
Context-shaped, 1
Copula, 55
Coup d'état, 18
Cross of gold, 34
Costs, defined, 136
Cuba, 46

D

Danes, 37
Deductive argument, 53
Deductive propositions, 52
Democratic logic, 93, 104
Democratic theory, 95
Dependency Theory, 22
Desires, defined, 7
Disjunctive Syllogism, 67
Dominant ideology, 82, 84
Dominant ruling class, 82-84

E

Eastern European bloc (former), 45
Education, 134
E-form proposition, 57
Egocentric predicament, 81

Eidos, 80
English civil wars, 41
Entertainment information, 110
Esperanto, 135
Ethnic Arithmetic, 44
Ethnicity (variable), 36
Europe(an), 23-24, 34, 37-38, 125
European-American(s), 36-37
Exchange Structure, defined, 3, 7-8
Existential quantifier, 60
External representation, defined, 40

F

Fallacy of Affirming the Consequence, 65
Fallacy of Denying the Antecedent, 66
Federalist Number 10, 106
Feedback, 18
Finns/Finnish, 37
Foreign aid, 22
Foreign exchange, 11
Foreign reparative redistribution, 22
France, 35, 38, 45
Free information, notion of, 115
Functional Relations, 3, 51, 87-88

G

Gender (variable), 38
General Agreement on Tariffs and Trade (GATT), 22

Germany, 45
Ghana, 19, 23
Global exchange, 11, 20, 22
Global justice, 20, 22
Government communication model, 127
Great Britain, 33, 38, 42

H
Hershey's, 19
History, 113
Hypothetical Syllogism, 66, 86

I
Idea, 80
Ideational Structure, defined, 3, 89
Idein, 80
I-form proposition, 57
Income level (variable), 37
Index of class voting, 33
Individual constants, 59
Individual variable, 59
Inductive propositions, 52
Information, defined, 109, 142
Information State, defined, 4
Information superhighway, 10
Information, types, 111
Infotainment, 110
Inherent needs, 15
Instantiation, 59
Internal representation, defined, 40
International exchange, 11, 19
International Monetary Fund (IMF), 20, 26
International politics, defined, ix
Irish Seanad (Senate), 44
Issues (variable), 34

J
Jews, 43

K
Knowledge, defined, 4
Kuwait, 66

L
Labor unions, 106-107
Latin American, 125
Leaks, defined, 109, 126
Leaks, typology of, 126
Lebanon, 44
Legislation, 76
Liverpool, 24

M
Marginal rate of substitution, defined, 8
Market, defined, 14
Maronite Christian, 44
Metaknowledge, defined, 4

Modus Ponens, 64, 86
Modus Tollens, 65
Multinational corporations (MNCs), 25-27
Mutual reciprocity, 15

N
NAACP, 66
Nantes, 24
Necessities, defined, 7
Needs, defined, 7
Neocolonial(ism), 45
New England, 44
New World Order, 10
New York, 38, 44
Newell and Stutman's research, 74
No distribution proposition, 56
Non-governmental agencies (NGOs), 27
North American Free Trade Association (NAFTA), 22, 98
North Carolina, 8
North-South Conflict, 25
Norwegians, 37

O
O-form proposition, 58
Optimization of gratification, 30

P
Participation Framework, defined, 4
Particular Affirmative, 55-56

Particular Negative, 55-56
Particular Quantity, 55
Participatory logic, 92
Particularistic standard, 31
Party affiliation (variable), 33
Party differential, defined, 132
People's candidate, 10
Polish, 37
Political action committees (PACs), 17
Political context, x, 3
Political domains, 1
Political exchange, defined, 7
Political ideology (variable), 34
Political Theory, defined, ix
Pork-barrel, defined, 102
Possible contextual influences, 1
Positive-sum game, 9
Predicate term, 58
Premise, defined, 52-53
Principle of Excluded Middle, 55
Principle of Identity, 55
Principle of Noncontradiction, 55
Propositional functions, 59
Propositions (basic types), 52-53
Prussian Germany, 45
Psycho-cultural connection, 104
Public administration, defined, ix
Public policy, defined, ix
Put on hold (strategy), 76

Q

Quantification Theory, 58
Quantification Theory Array, 61

R

Radical group, 83
Rational abstention, 39
Reaffirmation, 76
Remediation, 76
Representation, defined, 40, 97
Representative, defined, 40
Representative logic, 96
Representative Democracy, defined, x, 91, 94
Representing, defined, 40
Riksdag (Swedish Parliament), 46
Roman Catholics, 43
Rules of inference, 58
Ruling ideas, 82
Russia, 45

S

Self-preservation, 15, 18
Self-sustainability, 15
Shi'ite Muslims, 44
Social class, 33
Social contract, 41
Social group membership (variable), 33
Sought-for data, 116
Southern Europe(ans), 45
Soviet Union (former), 45
Spain, 45
Square Array, 63
Square of Opposition, 58, 61, 63
State, defined, 15, 18
State of affairs, 53
Steady state period, 33
Stock exchange, 11
Stock Issues Approach, 77
Structural Adjustment Programmes (SAPs), 19
Subject term, 58
Sun King, 45
Sunni Muslims, 44
Supreme Soviet(s), 45-46
Sweden/Swedish,37, 46
Switzerland, 38
Synthesis, 81
Systems Approach, 78

T

Theoretical framework, 1-2
Thesis, 80
Times Mirror Center, 97-98
Topic Relations, 3, 51, 88
Trade defined, 17
True propositions, 53-54
Truth and falsity, 53-54
Truth experts, 109
Turkish, 37
Twenty-Sixth Amendment to the United States Constitution, 37

U

Underdevelopment, 33
Unequal exchange, 19

United Nations General
 Assembly (UNGA), 27
United Nations Security
 Council (UNSC), 27
United States, 19, 33-38,
 43-44, 73, 96, 103-104,
 108, 119, 125, 138
Universal Affirmative,
 55-56
Universal Declaration of
 Human Rights (UDHR),
 25
Universal needs, 15
Universal Negative,
 55-56
Universal quantifier, 60
Universal quantity, 55
Universalistic standard, 31
Utility income, defined, 133

V

Venn Diagrams, 56
Voting, defined, 32, 93
Voting Rights Act of 1965
 (United States), 36

W

Washington, DC, 86
Washington Post, The, 102
Wants, defined, 7
West Africa, 44
West Virginia, 101
Western Europe(ans), 22, 33,
 95, 103-104
Western (super) powers, 26
White Anglo-Saxon
 Protestants
 (WASPS), 43
White House, 93

White Papers, 109
World Bank, 18, 20, 26
World War I, II, 47-48

Y

Yugoslavs, 37

Z

Zero-sum game, 8

About the Authors

Bangura, Abdul Karim teaches Political Science, SPSS and SAS Computer Programming and Analysis at Bowie State University. He holds a G.Dpl. in the Social Sciences from Stockholms Universitet in Sweden, a Ph.D. in Political Science from Howard University, a Ph.D. in Policy Sciences (emphasis in Development Economics) from the University of Maryland Baltimore Graduate School, and a Ph.D. in Linguistics from Georgetown University.

Isayas, Dawit teaches Philosophy and Logic at Bowie State University. He is a Doctoral Candidate in African Studies and Research at Howard University.

Smith, Gerald teaches Political Science and International Studies at Bowie State University. He received his Ph.D. in African Studies and Research from Howard University.

Thomas, Michael O. Rev. teaches Philosophy and Logic at Bowie State University. He got his Ph.D. in Theology at the United Theological Seminary in Dayton, Ohio.